Threading the Concept

Powerful Learning for the Music Classroom

Debra Gordon Hedden

With contributions by
Valerie Anne Baker and David L. Gadberry

Published in partnership with
MENC: The National Association for Music Education

ROWMAN & LITTLEFIELD EDUCATION
A division of
ROWMAN & LITTLEFIELD PUBLISHERS, INC.
Lanham • New York • Toronto • Plymouth, UK

Published in partnership with MENC: The National Association for Music Education

Published by Rowman & Littlefield Education
A division of Rowman & Littlefield Publishers, Inc.
A wholly owned subsidary of The Rowman & Littlefield Publishing Group, Inc.
4501 Forbes Boulevard, Suite 200, Lanham, Maryland 20706
http://www.rowmaneducation.com

Estover Road, Plymouth PL6 7PY, United Kingdom

British Library Cataloguing in Publication Information Available

Library of Congress Cataloging-in-Publication Data

Hedden, Debra Gordon, 1951–
    Threading the concept : powerful learning for the music classroom / Debra Gordon Hedden.
        p. cm.
    ISBN 978-1-60709-440-1 (cloth : alk. paper) — ISBN 978-1-60709-441-8 (pbk. : alk. paper) — ISBN 978-1-60709-442-5 (electronic)
    1. Music—Instruction and study. 2. School music—Instruction and study. I. Title.
    MT1.H39 2010
    780.71—dc22   2010015932

∞ ™ The paper used in this publication meets the minimum requirements of American National Standard for Information Sciences—Permanence of Paper for Printed Library Materials, ANSI/NISO Z39.48-1992.

Printed in the United States of America

CONTENTS

PREFACE

The purpose of this book is to offer the planning and delivery of music education in schools in a way that provides for deep learning for the students. There are a variety of methodologies and approaches that are focused on a particular premise; for instance, the Kodály method stresses a cappella singing and music literacy, the Orff approach focuses on active student involvement in music making through speech and ensemble activity, the Gordon method enhances accuracy in singing due to its emphasis on audiation, and the Dalcroze approach is devoted to eurhythmics.

Each of these methods or approaches is distinct and appropriate. In fact, the reader will note that every lesson plan in this book offers glimpses of these methods in a variety of ways. While each approach is valuable and fully endorsed by the author, this book is designed to skim the best of all approaches and methods and assimilate these in a way that allows for a focused lesson based on specific objectives, appropriate vocabulary, rehearsal of the concept, learning experiences devoted to deep learning, and consistent student involvement.

This approach is unique and allows each lesson to essentially "bombard" the learner with one concept, having the student sing, play, move, listen, read and write, and improvise and compose in small doses to learn the concept in myriad ways. The author subscribes to the idea that students learn in a multitude of ways and must have many experiences in order to truly learn musical concepts. Thus, the book provides information about pedagogy (the art/science of teaching—how to teach) and methodology (what to teach).

CHAPTER ONE
WE ARE WHAT WE HAVE LEARNED TO BE

T his book is devoted to delivering instruction in the music classroom in a unique fashion, one that is quite different from the
manner in which most music educators have been trained. Its
contents are intended for the person who is preparing to be a teacher as
well as the experienced teacher; however, each may view this with differ-
ing perspectives.

Because the contents offer a unique approach, the subject of threading
deserves preparatory discussion. Therefore, the reader should understand
that the following argument begins with the larger picture, that of philosophy and curriculum, and then proceeds to the smaller picture, that of
delivering specific lessons.

It is important to recognize that philosophy, curriculum, lesson planning, and lesson delivery are inextricably related. In addition, it is important to consider not only the ways in which children learn, but also the
way the learning is delivered by the teacher. Thus, the discussion must
attend to these components and will do so in a particular sequence.

There are several premises on which this book is based, all of which
must be considered in light of offering a music program that is intentionally mindful of best practice. Those premises are as follows:

1. The curriculum is comprised of conceptual learning experiences that include singing, performing, listening, moving,
   reading and writing, and improvising, composing, and creating music.

2. Learning is the result of myriad experiences through the acquisition of percepts that lead to conceptual knowledge, all accomplished through intentionally designed musical experiences that offer the students many ways to learn.

3. The teacher must be cognizant of the learning modes of the students and present learning experiences that are aural, visual, and kinesthetic in order to meet all students' needs.

4. Students' learning needs include a sequence of learning experiences that are first active in nature to allow the children to *do* music; next, the experiences include pictures of the concepts; and finally, the symbols of music are utilized to teach students to read and write music.

5. Learning experiences that are holistic allow the students to learn inductively and deductively, engaging all of the brain in taking in and processing music.

6. The concerted planning and delivery of music experiences that are connected to one particular concept at a time can facilitate deep learning and ultimately lead to the students' musical independence.

The following presents arguments for delivering music learning experiences that attend to learners' needs, that allow the learners to engage in active music making, that facilitate connected learning experiences to enhance and deepen the learning, and that offer different ways of experiencing music to motivate learners and to allow them to acquire skills and competencies in music. Let the journey begin!

Premise I: Curriculum Is Comprised of Conceptual Learning Experiences

Every music teacher delivers a program based on a philosophy of music education, whether or not it is articulated in written form. That philosophy is communicated both explicitly through the program's content and implicitly through particular emphases that the teacher practices. Thus, the very way in which a program is delivered, the learners who are participatory in that program, and the learning outcomes that are accomplished, are the result of the philosophical beliefs to which the teacher subscribes. According to Hodges (2000a), the idea that every person has some capacity for music is quite a different philosophy than the idea of providing music only to those who exhibit talent or can afford to learn music.

Both Reimer's (2003) philosophical posture toward aesthetic education and Elliott's (1995) view of music as an active learning medium demonstrate the range of expectations, beliefs, and practices that a teacher can embrace. The content we teach, the manner in which we teach, the emphases we place on particular aspects of the program, and the outcomes our students take away are all evidence of our philosophies.

It is not uncommon for teachers to practice the philosophies of their teachers, for we tend to teach the way we have been taught. The philosophy that is espoused by the teacher will directly impact the music curriculum, the learning outcomes and competencies, and, most likely, the attitudes of the learners.

Given that there are many different philosophies that support music education curricula, and ultimately, music education programs, a noticeable disparity exists in the quality of our programs and in the amount and kind of learning our students accrue. A continuum best describes the foci of programs, from that of facilitating full literacy for students exiting the program to that of consistent rote performances, many of which provide a trophy.

I would suggest that true quality in programs may fall somewhere in the middle with a balance of literacy, performance, creation of music, and many experiences leading to a wide palette of listening repertoire. More specifically, that the students have become independent musicians once they have left a program is evidence that there has been an effective balance of skills, behaviors, and repertoire that allows them to function without us.

Certainly, in the general music classroom we might agree that one of the goals is to offer students a wealth of learning experiences with music in a variety of ways. Both the breadth and variety of those experiences forge one aspect of this book, for one of the foci is in creating curricular inclusions that embrace daily experiences in singing, performing, moving, creating (improvising or composing), reading and writing, and listening to music.

These experiences allow the child to build a repertoire through consistent but brief listening experiences. In addition, skills, knowledge, and behaviors are acquired through *doing* music by singing, performing, moving, and creating. Boardman (2001) states that "music is indeed a physical phenomenon; without the presence of sound, music simply would not exist" (p. 47). Thus, using music in all learning activities in the music classroom seems not only appropriate, but also necessary.

In a given class period of thirty to forty minutes, it is possible to offer lessons that include all of these elements, all in small doses so that the children are not overwhelmed and so that the teacher can successfully maintain motivation and classroom management. I will argue that we often ignore many of these kinds of experiences as children mature, and that we place focus on one or two aspects of music rather than helping them to become more well-rounded musicians.

Thus, I would support the idea that all music programs in the preK–12 setting consider the idea of offering curricula that include a wealth of musical experiences regardless of the particular music discipline. That listening, moving, singing, performing, reading and writing, and creating should be relegated only to general music is severely limiting what older students can do and profoundly constrains music learning opportunities.

The premise of this book is to organize learning experiences in such a way that the learner maximizes his or her potential to learn through different kinds of experiences. This does not mean that it is haphazard and the result is a mishmash of activities, but rather that it is a carefully crafted curriculum that allows the learner to engage in music learning that is organized differently from existing methods. To do this, the larger picture of the total curriculum is important to ponder, and the context in which the curriculum is delivered is noteworthy.

It is important to understand that a curriculum should include both musical content and behavioral elements, for it is impossible to teach children to sing, perform, move, create, read and write, and listen well without teaching them how to handle themselves, how to meet the teacher's expectations, how to be responsible and make good choices, and how to work as a team. While it is essential to place responsibility on the learners, the teacher is the adult who is charged with the task of providing learning experiences; thus he or she must have a clear picture of the learning that is to be accomplished throughout the year, both musically and behaviorally, and help students attain that learning. The responsibility rests both on the teacher and the students.

Let me illustrate this further. In the contained classroom, the teacher typically works with twenty-five students during the entire day. In that setting, each student competes only against him- or herself for individual grades in math, language arts, science, and social studies. But in the music classroom, the environment is very different. The product of the music classroom is one that is communal, requiring everyone to work together. While individual learning and assessment occur, the final product is often a group endeavor; hence, teaching children to be responsible, respectful, and cooperative is a necessary part of any music classroom.

The idea of the students learning responsibility and cooperation is even more important when we consider that many music classrooms are much larger than twenty-five students, and that the classes change every twenty, thirty, or forty-five minutes throughout the day. Later, the topic of classroom management will be further explored. For now, let us return to larger context, that of learning in the music classroom.

Learning is the primary objective related to concerted planning and delivery of instruction by the music educator. The macro view of learning experiences is termed *curriculum*, or the general plan for the duration of the semester or year. Curriculum encompasses the *scope* of the concepts (e.g., melody, harmony, rhythm, and form) and their graduated increase of sophistication at each grade level, and the *sequence*, or the order in which the concepts and their subconcepts are introduced at each grade level.

For example, introducing rhythm to kindergarten children may be accomplished through saying their names and clapping the long and short sounds that indicate the pattern; by first grade, the children can read quarter notes, quarter rests, and paired eighth notes, particularly through designating quarter notes as "walking" and eighth notes as "running." The sequence accommodates elaboration, further exploration of the concept, and more opportunities to learn rhythm through reading, writing, performing, singing, listening, and creating.

The scope and sequence of the curriculum is a *carefully articulated plan* that defines the learning experiences throughout the program. It specifies the conceptual learning experiences, connects particular literature to the concepts, and integrates behavioral aspects so that the students can function in the classroom setting and grow in their musicianship. Abeles, Hoffer, and Klotman (1994) offer particular ideas for curriculum consideration in the form of guidelines. Curriculum should be:

1. Educational, meaning that the learners acquire skills, comprehension, and attitudes through music learning experiences;

2. Valid, referring to music as a core part of the school curriculum involving its own "field of study" (p. 278);

3. Fundamental, meaning that basic concepts are taught through music, rather than as mere facts about music;

4. Representative, or offering learning experiences that include all kinds of music to allow the learner to have a breadth of knowledge and skills—varieties of styles, periods, and genres;

5. Contemporary, meaning that currency of music is also important to include in the curriculum;

6. Relevant, regarding the "interests and needs of the students" (p. 279) so that the teacher can engage the learners and facilitate learning through current music that can be related to other music; and

7. Learnable, or content that is based on age and developmentally appropriate criteria for the students.

A curriculum predicated on these guidelines would indeed be broad in scope and well designed in terms of sequential learning for students at any age. The learners would be actively engaged in making music and would gain knowledge and skill about music, with music, and through music. Hence, this curricular approach would be classified as being experiential, or experience-based.

In general music in particular, it is apparent that textbook series and current methods of teaching may focus primarily on a selected group of concepts, sometimes limiting exposure to others and sometimes avoiding varieties of literature. Those curricula may be appealing; however, the teacher is cautioned about the limitations, for these do affect the scope of learning.

The ideas in this book represent an *eclectic* approach, one that utilizes elements of several methods and approaches to general music. The eclectic approach may be considered by some to be piecemeal in nature, but a strong argument can be made that it attends to all kinds of learners due to its inclusion of several ways of learning music.

Kassner (2009) points to the value of eclecticism by saying that it "connotes using different approaches, not necessarily including all approaches at any one given time" (p. 63). He maintains that an eclectic approach allows the teacher various teaching venues rather than becoming landlocked with a single approach. Because the eclectic teacher draws upon many sources and utilizes different pedagogies, learning can be both broader and deeper (Kassner, 2009).

I would argue that the eclectic approach can be termed the *electric* method because its central theme is presenting learning through a variety of modes, through engaging the learner in myriad ways to make and experience music, and through numerous ways of motivating the learner by recognizing his or her preferences for learning rather than the teacher's chosen mode.

This approach may be attractive to the teacher because it utilizes many kinds of learning, includes all kinds of literature, and allows the learner to acquire comprehension, skills, and behaviors that are broad-based. The remainder of this book will be devoted to presenting the ideas of learning and teaching through a perspective that is not only unique, but also reflective of eclecticism for all of those reasons.

The Music Educators National Conference (MENC) initially published *The Eclectic Curriculum in American Music Education: Contributions of Dalcroze, Kodály, and Orff* (Carder, 1990) in the early 1970s, focusing on curriculum. In contrast, the ideas described in this book do not outline a curriculum, but rather an approach to lesson design and implementation that serves as a template *on which* to build a curriculum.

Thus, while the eclectic approach is not new, the manner in which it is designed in this book appears to be distinctive. The following is an attempt to make a case for learning that is deep, occurs through a variety of ways, and centers on one concept. To do that, let us first focus further on how students learn.

CHAPTER TWO
LEARNING AND THINKING

I t is important to consider the ways in which children learn and think in order to plan and deliver instruction that facilitates optimal learning. When children succeed, they usually are motivated to continue to learn; thus the cycle is a critical one for our classrooms. Let's take a look at the ideas regarding learning and thinking from the macro perspective first.

Premise II: Learning Results from Percepts and Concepts

Children learn music in a variety of ways. First, they are exposed to hearing music, then to responding to it physically, and finally they learn by engaging in activities during music instruction. Through musical experiences, percepts are formed and serve as a direct conduit to the formation of concepts, given sufficient and effective experiences. Those percepts are acquired through singing, listening, moving, and using body percussion and simple unpitched percussion instruments in the preschool and early primary grades—a true example of experiential learning.

As the child matures, the teacher begins to include general learning about melody such as teaching the children to identify high and low sounds in a song and same and different parts of a song. These experiences pave the way for more specific learning such as high, middle, and low pitches; discrete pitches of the song; phrases that are identical or different; and overall form, such as verse and refrain. The sequence from percept to concept is important and requires that the teacher deliver lessons that are developmentally appropriate.

Merriam-Webster defines the term *concept* as "something conceived in the mind . . . an abstract or generic idea generalized from particular instances" (online). Bergethon, Boardman, and Montgomery (1997) suggest that the curriculum is based on "essential concepts and principles that constitute the structure of the subject area" (p. 5).

The four main concepts in music are melody, harmony, rhythm, and form, with all others (e.g., articulation and dynamics) serving as subconcepts related to each of these. Concepts are actually abstract in nature, meaning that you cannot reach out and touch them, but can think about them. The learner must have sufficient time and experience with the idea of the concept before he or she is able to demonstrate command of the concept. Therefore, varied and diverse learning is required prior to the acquisition of conceptual learning.

Preceding abstract thinking and cognition, concrete experiences are necessary for children to be equipped with appropriate contexts for learning abstract processes later on. In those concrete experiences, children sing, move, listen, read and write, perform, and create music from the simplest forms to increasingly more complex formats.

If children have myriad experiences with music, they develop perceptions (e.g., that the melody has different sounds), and these ultimately lead to conceptual learning such as high/low, higher than/lower than, and ascending/descending sounds that the child can identify, replicate, read, and create. Thus, perception must precede conception, and both ways of knowing require that the learner be involved in *doing* music through learning experiences that allow him or her to take in information

1. through the senses (seeing, hearing, feeling);

2. through performance of music by singing, moving, reading musical icons, and creating;

3. through listening to develop the ear and to assist in acquiring a musical palette of sounds and performance practices, and in acquiring aural acuity skills to distinguish different voices, instruments, and ensembles; and

4. through careful and sequential instruction that enables the assemblage of concrete experiences to underlie abstract, conceptual knowledge.

Carlsen (1973) refers to three types of thinking that lead to knowing, all of which apply to knowing about music. The first is discrimination, which is the basis of thinking, referring to the ability to recognize and understand that things are different. That differences are the crux of discrimination is important to learning music, for the learner must be able to distinguish high from low, loud from soft, fast from slow, and sound from silence.

Second, sequence learning requires that there be a certain order to things such as events or objects. For example, the sequence of a song allows the learner to know that the order consists of the introduction, the verse, the refrain, and the coda. And last, concept formation requires many opportunities to learn through discrimination and sequence in order that the learner can "classify otherwise dissimilar objects or events" (Carlsen, 1973, p. 36).

An example of concept formation is teaching steady beat over a period of many kinds of lessons and then introducing the rhythm of the words, ultimately having some children perform steady beat while the others perform the rhythm of the song. The concept of rhythm and its subconcept, steady beat, while related, are certainly not synonymous, but present difficulty for children when they are asked to distinguish between the two. For children to accurately identify, perform (sans teacher modeling), and use steady beat and rhythm, they must be able to employ their conceptual knowledge.

Learning is a complex subject; therefore there are many theories that have shaped the manner in which we currently think about learning. One approach to dissecting the kinds of learning that might occur is through the cognitive (knowledge), affective (preferences and attitudes), and psychomotor (physical skill) domains. These refer to the particular way in which learning is classified, each of which contributes to specific aspects of learning.

Cognitive learning was categorized in one way by Benjamin Bloom, a faculty member at the University of Chicago, beginning in 1944. He based his work on the premise that educational objectives that are operationalized exist in a hierarchy from the simplest learning experiences to the most complex, each of which is dependent on the command of all preceding levels of learning.

Bloom's Taxonomy, as it is called, not only identified six categories of cognitive learning on which to base learning objectives, but also allowed the assessment of learning at each level to be accomplished through the criteria of the objectives. Bloom focused on the importance of each student's ability to achieve learning at all levels, and advocated that immediate feedback and correction frequently occur for each student (Eisner, 2000).

The most basic level of learning in Bloom's Taxonomy is knowledge; it is observable when a student identifies, recognizes, or defines that which he or she is asked to do. Presenting the symbol of a quarter note would allow students to identify what it is or that it is worth one beat. The second level of the taxonomy is comprehension, accomplished through explanation, demonstration, or interpretation. Using the quarter note, comprehension could be noted through a student's demonstration of clapping quarter notes as he or she reads them on the board.

The third level is application and is characterized by classifying, applying, and sequencing information. The quarter note might be the basis of rhythmic writing by the third-grade class, with the teacher asking students to write a measure in 4/4 that has four beats and includes two quarter notes, ultimately performing the rhythm for the class. The students would need to *apply* their knowledge of different notes' duration, of how to write the notes, and how to perform the rhythm correctly.

At the fourth level, analysis occurs when children can discriminate, analyze, and compare. If the teacher were to present examples of the third-grade rhythms, using an incorrect example, he or she would ask the students to "eyeball" a pattern and determine if it had the correct number of beats. He or she might then ask them how to correct the rhythm so that only four beats were there, thus having them analyze.

The fifth level, synthesis, comprises assembling or creating something new from old knowledge. For instance, if the third-grade class were to use a 4/4 meter to create a four-measure song that demonstrated their ability to accurately use quarter, half, and eighth notes, they would have offered evidence of synthesis. Synthesis involves creation, composition, and formulation. The sixth level is evaluation and refers to judging, rating, and evaluating. It implies that the learner has developed sufficient skill to have a criterion in mind. Thus, asking the third-grade class to read a new song in 4/4 that includes several quarter notes and to evaluate if they correctly read the rhythm is an example of this level of knowledge. Bloom, Engle-hart, Furst, Hill, and Krathwohl (1956) referred to the first two levels as lower-order thinking skills (LOTS) and the upper four levels as higher-order thinking skills (HOTS), maintaining that HOTS cannot be learned until LOTS are sufficiently learned.

Using Krathwohl, Bloom, and Masia's (1964) Affective Taxonomy to address preferences and attitudes is also a consideration that teachers might make in attending to these aspects of music learning. In this taxonomy, level 1 is receiving, or sharing and listening, a critical element for music programs. Level 2 is responding, or approving or expressing acclaim. In the third level, valuing allows the students to support, refute, and appreciate, thus demonstrating that there is basis for justification of such responses.

Level 4 involves organizing, characterized as defining or formulating. And level 5 is characterizing, meaning that a rating may be used with respect to offering ideas for revision. As Labuta and Smith (1997) suggest, using the Affective Taxonomy in behavioral terms and then measuring learning is a difficult process, but worthy of contemplation when planning music instruction.

And finally, the Psychomotor Taxonomy (Simpson, 1966) recognizes seven levels of classification: (a) perception, or using the senses to take in information; (b) set, to be ready and prepared for a performance; (c) guided response, or learning by trial and error (this is sometimes referred to as heuristics); (d) mechanism or automatic response, or responding through habitual practice; (e) complex overt response, comprised of demonstrating performance with skill and coordination; (f) adaptation, or adjusting the performance to fit the requirements of the setting; and (g) origination, or integrating a newly added aspect to the performance.

All three taxonomies are pertinent to music. Because music is learned cognitively, we need to consider the specifics in planning instruction; we also need to contemplate the affective elements in music, for we tend to respond to it based on our preferences and perform with expressivity according to our own interpretations. The technical or mechanical aspects are essential to performance, although it would seem that these are more appropriate for specific ensemble and solo work.

Certainly, singing, movement, performance on instruments, and reading and writing music require different degrees of these levels and should also be considered as integral to music instruction.

Premise III: Learning Experiences Should Meet Students' Needs

We know that children learn in different ways, that they soak up information through their senses, and that they are typically first visual learners as babies, but also absorb auditorily (hearing) and kinesthetically (feeling through large motor movements). James and Galbraith (1985) describe sensory learning as perceptual modalities, commenting that these are the means through which information is "extracted from the environment by the senses" (p. 20).

There is a dominant modality that serves as the conduit for information to be assimilated through "sensory channel[s]" as the child acquires information (Barbe and Milone, 1980, p. 45). Barbe, Swassing, and Milone (1979) identified learning modalities as visual, auditory, and kinesthetic, with combinations of these as the fourth classification. The auditory modality is prevalent among primary learners, and the employment of different modalities occurs through gradual emergence of those modalities with maturation (Barbe and Milone, 1980).

To illustrate the differences, a hypothetical situation might be useful. For instance, if I were to invite you for dessert next Sunday and needed to provide you with directions to my house, would you prefer that I tell you the directions (auditory), draw you a map (visual), or use both? Each of us has developed a primary way to take in specific information; however, it is plausible that that preference changes with the kind of information that is available and/or the task that is required.

Further exploration of this topic is warranted, for it may help us to better understand both the learning process and product in our classrooms. Several studies have reported that concerted attention to delivering lessons via different learning modalities is critical to reaching our students and facilitating maximum learning. While the studies mentioned below are not fully representative of all those conducted, they do present interesting findings worth considering:

- Success in learning may be more readily attained for those with predispositions for mixed modalities over single sensory approaches (Barbe and Milone, 1981) or "visual language" (Wilson, 1996, p. 2).

- Underachieving learners preferred the kinesthetic mode (Dunn, 1993); average children were predominately visual learners

(Dunn, 1993); males were more frequently kinesthetic, and females were more auditory (Dunn, 1993; Restak, 1979); however, Barbe and Milone (1981) did not identify differences between males and females.

- Among K–12 students in a large study conducted by Specific Diagnostic Studies, 29 percent learned primarily through visual means, 34 percent via auditory presentation, and 37 percent through kinesthetic mode (cited by Willis and Hodson, 1999), but Barbe, Swassing, and Milone (1979) reported different results, that approximately 30 percent of learners were visual, 25 percent were auditory, 15 percent were kinesthetic, and 30 percent were combinations of these.

What is most important about this information is the impact the delivery of learning has upon the learner. Overall, the research suggests that the teacher's ability to offer learning through a number of modes improves motivation and achievement, a point worth great consideration. If the teacher is able to deliver instruction that is matched to the *learners'* preferred styles or modalities, there is a significant chance that learning is accomplished and allows for further motivation to continue to learn.

Bargar, Bargar, and Cano (1994) maintain that teachers need to be cognizant of *their* learning modalities because these ultimately affect their approaches to teaching and attitudes toward their learners, often demonstrating a focus on the teacher's strengths in learning rather than considering what is best for the students' learning.

In the larger picture, teachers are products of school systems and have been trained similarly. Schools are typically focused on delivering learning that is biased in favor of one kind of learner (Willis and Hodson, 1999). As teachers, we must consider the learners' best interests and develop curricula and learning experiences that are going to reach the students. Therefore, it is the teacher who must adapt to the students' needs rather than the students adapting to the teacher's preferences.

Based on the results of some studies (Barbe and Milone, 1981; Sanders, 1996), it is recommended that learning be delivered through the student's primary modality and reinforced with weaker ones. This implies that the teacher present lessons visually, auditorily, and kinesthetically (Miller, 2002), suggesting that the multisensory approach may expedite learning because the learner can see, hear, and physically feel or perform the construct, which may translate as quicker and deeper understanding.

"Children retain 24 percent of what they hear, 40 percent of what they see, and 70 percent of what they learn through multisensory experiences" (Mann, 1989, cited by Collett, 1991, p. 42). Further corroboration of this is reported by Persellin's (1992) work in the music classroom. Her results suggest that multimodal instruction did not impede learners, noting the focus of auditory and kinesthetic approaches in Orff, Dalcroze, and Kodály classrooms.

Premise IV: Generative Learning Is Enactive, Iconic, and Symbolic

As Jerome Bruner (1966) and others have maintained, the generative approach to learning is necessary and efficient in accommodating conceptual learning through construction of meaning. It is comprised of three levels of learning that are sequential and developmentally appropriate.

First, children participate in active learning—that is, they *do* singing, moving, listening, performing, and creating of music; a term to which Bruner refers is "enactive" learning (as opposed to "inactive," which means they are not doing anything). They are involved in doing music, learning perceptually from a wealth of experiences, such as playing body percussion to learn steady beat and rhythmic patterns or learning actions with a simple song that helps them remember the sequence of several verses.

Enactive learning is largely physical and allows the brain to employ muscle memory as a means of remembering and learning. It is also a means of creating awareness of the musical concepts—for instance, that in playing steady beat, the child performs a consistent tap on the hand drum in a repeated motion, thus learning through concrete experience. Pairing the awareness factor with muscle memory is a primary way of learning for young children, but also may be a chief mode of learning for many adults.

The second approach to generative learning is integrating the visual aspect—iconic learning, that of pictures of a particular concept (such as melody, harmony, rhythm, or form) that enable the children to learn visually. The textbooks offer a wide array of icons ranging from pictures of red hearts, to show beat to stair steps to show what a scale looks like, to sophisticated rhythmic patterns with dots and dashes on matrices to indicate rhythmic canons. Given that children are naturally drawn to pictures in storybooks and games, iconic presentation is quite easy for them to understand. It is visual presentation of the concept in its clearest form.

The third and final step in generative learning is highly complex, difficult, and requires a great deal of musical experiences before successful transfer occurs. Symbolic learning relates to just that; symbols represent an abstract idea, such as a treble clef standing for sounds that are pitched from middle C upward on a keyboard.

Symbolic learning is totally abstract, removed from the "thing" it represents, and is difficult to learn due to that abstraction. Children around the age of nine years old are capable of simple abstractions, so some symbolic learning can occur around that time and very limited symbolic presentation might be integrated in grades 1 and 2.

There are three kinds of symbols that children learn during their formal education. First, they learn letters of the alphabet in which a sound is associated with each letter. Subsequently, they learn to string letters together to form words, a further abstraction from the "thing" being represented. The letters are then put in sequences for phrases and sentences to make meaning out of the strings.

As an example, a child learns to make the sounds for the letters *c*, *a*, and *t*, later to put these together to form the word *cat*, an abstract symbol that represents a four-legged animal that purrs. The child then learns to use the word in the proper context of a sentence or question. Further abstraction occurs when capital letters and punctuation are added and must be comprehended during reading.

Numbers are the second set of symbols with which children are confronted. They first memorize them, then learn to count, and eventually learn that other symbols such as plus and minus signs, division brackets, and multiplication signs designate particular functions. In a simple division problem of 12 divided by 3, there are a variety of symbols and calculations that occur, further complicating the mere numbers.

The abstract concept that 12 of something is divided by 3 of something is challenging. But the use of dividing 12 by 3, then multiplying the product by the divisor, subtracting it from the dividend, and identifying a remainder is a significant operation of symbols. Typically, the iconic representation is absent from this kind of learning, often forcing memorization to occur before conceptual understanding does.

The symbols that represent sound and silence in music are yet another set of abstractions presented to children in their formative years.

The difficulty does not often lie in their ability to correctly read or notate a short rhythmic pattern, but to combine the duration aspects of rhythm with the pitch aspects of melody, and then relate these to a particular clef or instrument.

Essentially, several sets of information must mesh for success to occur in learning to read and notate even the simplest four-bar songs—that of melody and rhythm in tandem with that of words or language. In addition, the Italian terms that signify tempo, articulation, and dynamics are another layer of symbols for children to decipher.

What is stunning is that the three sets of symbols are usually presented all through elementary school years, placing quite a burden on the teacher and the student. For these to be learned and assimilated, careful instructional planning and delivery are critical components to the students' success. Thus, varied experiences that contribute to well-rounded musicians and musicianship consist of enactive and iconic learning in which to forge a path for symbolic learning to coalesce.

Boardman (2001) aptly captures the essence of learning in her statement that "music learning is the construction of musical meaning" (p. 52). This implies that the amalgam of music experiences that are concertedly taught concretely and abstractly allow the learner to know music, not know *about* music.

It would seem that the teacher must consider a variety of factors when planning instruction. Age appropriateness of curricula and learning experiences should serve as the center of instructional decisions, along with learning modalities that enable learners to maximize their knowledge and skill.

Premise V: Holistic Learning Experiences Engage the Entire Brain

Through holistic learning experiences, both sides of the brain engage in functioning, allowing thinking to occur both generally and specifically, inductively and deductively, and through verbal and logical means in tandem with intuitive, perceptual, and expressive venues. Music experiences that are multimodal (Hodges, 2000b; Paxcia-Bibbins, 1998) and multidimensional contribute to holistic learning, or that which provides brain processing in both hemispheres of the brain.

Boardman (2001) maintains that "music learning will occur only to the extent that music is experienced holistically," which requires a new way of organizing and delivering instruction (p. 52). Holistic learning is an active approach, but is not just a litany of activities.

Regelski (1983, 2004) cautions teachers that music activities do not necessarily provide conceptual learning. In fact, he notes that many teachers believe that the natural transfer of activities to concepts occurs easily; however, this does not appear to be the case. Children require *concerted* teaching of concepts that can occur through activities, but not be limited to the activity itself. They also need to be expertly guided in making connections among learning experiences.

To illustrate this point, introducing very high and low sounds on the keyboard to kindergarteners may be a part of several lessons, but will most likely remain isolated knowledge without specific and concerted connections forged by the teacher. He or she must revisit high and low sounds on other instruments to ensure the students can aurally identify them, then use the voice to perform high and low sounds through stories with sound effects. As the students acquire awareness, the introduction of high and low icons on the board that are visual, and are also presented with sound, is necessary.

Connecting the visual and auditory aspects is essential, for *music does not really exist without sound.* The teacher must present the iconic format of high and then *play* examples of high sounds for the children to form initial reference points. This, I believe, is a step we may often forget to include, perhaps because we, as teachers, know this, but our students do not.

Having the students read high and low icons and perform them vocally and on pitched instruments is an important step to cognition and to the transfer to symbols. Gradually substituting letter names for high sounds (e.g., high A) and low sounds (e.g., low B) and performing these facilitate music reading and understanding.

The difficult aspect of teaching music lies in the subtleties such as middle sounds. Children generally identify the extremes of high and low easily, but teaching less differentiated sounds, such as those in their singing range, is more challenging. Thus, the case for teaching children through concerted sequences of connected learning experiences that relate to each other is the key point. The bottom line is that we must consider not only what they learn, but also how they learn.

In conclusion, there are multiple aspects of learning that teachers must consider when planning and delivering instruction. These are essential to reaching students cognitively, but are also integral to their motivation to learn and to participate in music. The teacher is responsible for making decisions about learning and can offer learning experiences that assist the learner in acquiring attitudes, skills, and competencies that affect life-long learning and participation in music.

THE CONCEPT OF THREADING

The purpose of this book is to offer a pedagogical approach to teaching children, to teaching them music, and to teaching them first through experiences that create awareness and percepts, and finally, to teaching through conceptual learning. It is based on an approach that is enactive, focused on one concept at a time, and devoted to sensory learning—that is, hearing, seeing, feeling, and doing.

The reader must be cautioned that these experiences are not isolated activities, but rather are each one in a series of lessons that helps to employ lower-order thinking skills (LOTS) and higher-order thinking skills (HOTS), and includes enactive, iconic, symbolic, and holistic learning. These lessons do not suffice as a curriculum, but rather serve as *templates* for other lessons that would contribute to an entire curriculum.

Premise VI: Experiences Based on One Concept Enhance Learning

Let's explore the concept of threading. If we were to observe a fourth-grade science lesson focused on making a volcano in the classroom, we would notice that the objectives and goals are totally organized around that concept. The learning experience would be planned to instruct the students, guide their creation of the volcano, discuss the chemical reaction that occurs, and assess the students' ability to successfully complete the experiment. In other words, everything that took place during that class would be related to *one concept*. The teacher would not be teaching a little about volcanoes, then jump to another concept on weather, then to another on gravity, and so on.

It would be prudent to note that the science, language arts, and social studies textbooks for contained classrooms typically present lessons related to each other by concepts and lay out the lessons to address the concept in each lesson. Unfortunately, this seems to be quite different for music; some music lessons do jump from concept to concept within a class and the students are expected to be able to separate their experiences, recognize different concepts during various lessons, and apply that information in new contexts.

I will vigorously argue that the students are not necessarily able to separate the concepts within a class. Thus, the idea of threading one concept throughout each class becomes the ideal pedagogical strategy, in my opinion. This approach is effective when the concept is taught through many musical experiences, ultimately deepening the learning.

A Rationale for Including Many Musical Experiences in Each Class

A justification for including a composite of music learning experiences in every class or in every week focuses on singing, moving, listening, reading and writing, performing, and improvising and composing. A brief discussion of each one would be appropriate.

- *Singing.* For children to learn to use their internal instrument is essential, for they hear, feel, and manipulate their voices, learning to match pitch, control pitch and breath, and vocalize sounds with which to read and perform music.

- *Moving.* Some students learn primarily through physical engagement while others learn secondarily via physical experiences. Movement allows students to respond to and bodily create accompaniment to music. Muscle memory and internalization of music through movement facilitate powerful learning.

- *Listening.* If children are not afforded myriad opportunities to listen to a variety of styles, genres, and periods of music, they do not have a point of reference in hearing what is possible—what excellent voices sound like, what phenomenal instrumentalists can do, what beautiful phrasing and appropriate dynamics can lend to music, how harmony differs from melody, and much more. In short, if children are robbed of consistent learning experiences in listening, they do not know what quality music is beyond the level of what they are currently doing. Their skills are not likely to improve without those reference points.

- *Performing.* Children can learn simple accompaniment skills on unpitched percussion; can learn to play simple melodies on recorders; can learn to accompany themselves on Orff instruments, autoharps, ukuleles, and guitars; can learn to be independent musicians by reading music and tablatures; and can gain confidence by performing vocal and instrumental solos, both in small groups and in class ensembles.

- *Reading and writing.* When children learn to read and write the symbols of music, they have ownership of it and become independent musicians—skills they carry throughout life. Reading and writing allow children to manipulate the "language" (symbols) of music and assist in reducing the amount of rote teaching that can occur. Imagine children learning language by rote and never having opportunities to read and write. I doubt that we want to replicate that scenario in our music classrooms.

- *Improvising and composing.* Children are afforded opportunities to create music ranging from four-beat introductions to songs, from changing a few words of text to writing parodies of existing text, from writing three beats of dictation in first grade to composing songs in sixth grade. The manipulation or utilization of music improvisation and notation are essential to the child's understanding of how to apply sound to symbol, how to interpret the meaning of the composer from the child's view, and how to work with text and notation to form parts of a song or a whole piece.

The Concept of Threading

The idea of threading can be described as a way of connecting the content of a lesson just as a needle with thread connects one piece of fabric to another. Merriam-Webster (online) defines *thread* as an act of interweaving, creating the interspersion of the thread throughout an entity; more specifically, as "a line of reasoning or train of thought that connects the parts in a sequence (as of ideas or events)."

Threading a lesson can be translated as immersing the students in learning one concept in a variety of ways that bombard their senses of seeing, hearing, and feeling. Everything the students do within the lesson relates to *the concept*. They sing, perform, move, create, read and write, and listen with only that concept in mind, all others ignored for the moment so that there is no chance of confusing them. They learn by doing—that is, active engagement in the learning; they learn by seeing both iconically and symbolically; they learn by hearing the aural transmission of the music; they learn by singing and speaking the vocabulary term through oral transmission. And the result is a powerful, meaningful lesson that they will not forget because they sang, listened, performed, moved, created, and read and wrote the concept. Thus, the "concept can't be experienced; it *is* the experience" (Pearce, 1975, p. 224, as cited by Regelski, 1983, p. 57).

Threading a lesson is quite contrary to the way most of us have learned music or have been trained in teaching. In many classrooms, a variety of concepts may be explored in a given lesson, but without connections among these activities, learning is most likely minimal and may be perceived as "fluff." It might appear that the children are enjoying themselves and having fun, but not really learning other than through happenstance. While this is certainly not true in all instances, it may be in many.

In lesson planning, threading refers to the identification of one and only one concept for the entire lesson. For instance, if we were to plan for a second-grade general music class and identified the concept of tempo for a lesson or for a unit of instruction, tempo would be the commonality among all music experiences for those classes. We would temporarily suspend the integration of other concepts until the students had full grasp of the intended one, tempo.

As the students accrue learning, careful use of other concepts might occur within the context of this concept, but not initially or it will confuse them. They are not yet ready to separate the ideas of tempo from those of other concepts, so avoiding the confusion is a necessary element of planning instruction.

In planning lessons that include singing, performing, moving, creating, reading and writing, and listening, the concept of tempo would become the common element or thread of every segment. For instance, the vocabulary would be introduced to the class by saying one of the student's names with a slow tempo and a fast tempo. The students might be asked to offer ideas about things that have slow and fast tempi such as animals and modes of transportation.

The concept of tempo might then be further demonstrated through a listening lesson in which the tempo changes are obvious to allow students to form points of reference for *slow* and *fast*, such as Grieg's "In the Hall of the Mountain King." They could signal slow and fast tempi with different gestures, such as hands on their knees for slow and hands on their heads for fast.

A transition to reading music might be to rehearse the performing of quarter notes, half notes, and quarter rests that have been previously learned. These will later be found in the song the class learns. For now, the teacher helps the class to clap the rhythm in a steady, slow tempo, then adds a little quicker tempo for the second reading, and finally a fast tempo when the students have good command of accuracy in reading. The class is now primed for learning a song that contains these rhythms.

The teacher might sing directions in a slow and fast manner for the students to find a particular song in their textbooks. He or she might ask the class to read the rhythms of the first two staves, those that they just clapped, doing so with a slow tempo. As the class perfects this, he or she speeds up the tempo. Finally, he or she sings the entire song to them in a slow tempo and they learn it by phrases before singing the entire song together. He or she "plays" with it by changing the tempo each time they sing it, engaging the class in listening and following his or her tempi.

Next, the teacher instructs the class to carefully and quietly stand in front of their chairs to listen for directives for a tempo game. He or she tells them that he or she is going to play the song with a slow tempo at the keyboard while the class listens for the steady beat or tempo. The class is instructed to walk in any direction with two rules: they must keep their feet on the floor and they must not touch anybody or anything. He or she plays the song slowly with the students walking the tempo. When he or she stops, the class stops, for they respond to his or her *sound* cues.

The teacher then plays the song a bit quicker, having students match their steps to the tempo. He or she stops to let them clear their heads before moving to a fast tempo. But after a few seconds of the fast music, he or she needs to get them calmed and back to their seats, so he or she deliberately and consistently slows the tempo as they progress back to their chairs. They sit down, having responded physically to the tempo.

The teacher concertedly mentions that the class is ready to play unpitched percussion instruments to further learn about tempo. He or she is preventative in modeling how he or she wants the class to get the instruments—by walking with a slow tempo, getting the instrument with a slow tempo, walking back to their chairs with a slow tempo, and waiting patiently with no noise and no tempo until everyone has one and he or she is ready to tell them what they'll do next. They proceed in getting the instruments and wait for his or her instructions.

The teacher asks students to play a steady beat with his or her drum beat, modeling a slow tempo. As he or she continues, he or she asks them to play music that is slow but matches his or her steady beat—they create patterns using quarter and half notes. He or she then adds their rhythmic patterns to the song, utilizing their percussion accompaniment.

As they finish the song, the teacher asks them to follow his or her tempo change and he or she speeds up to a faster tempo. The class continues with quarter and half notes, but everyone is moving faster. He or she then invites them to sing with him or her as they play. He or she repeats this, but then concertedly slows the music and ends with a slow tempo.

Lastly, he or she moves back to the keyboard to play the bare chords of the song they learned, having the class improvise rhythms with his or her slow tempo and then his or her fast tempo. As he or she brings the song to a close, he or she gestures for everyone to stop, having the class rest their instruments in their laps. They are instructed to take a slow tempo to return the instruments.

As they complete this, the teacher brings the lesson to closure to recap what they have learned. He or she plays a steady beat on the keyboard and asks the first row to improvise a rhythm to match his or her slow tempo; then he or she asks the second row to improvise a rhythm to match the fast tempo. He or she instructs the class to signal whether he or she is now playing the song with a fast or slow tempo. Then he or she asks them to calmly blurt the new word they learned today. As he or she reminds them they learned *tempo*, he or she has them demonstrate a slow tempo as they walk to the door to be dismissed.

The long and short of this is that the entire lesson was focused on one vocabulary word, *tempo*, and all learning experiences involved using that word in the context of singing, playing, moving, listening, reading and writing, and creating. The lesson was introduced with the vocabulary and every element of it used visual, auditory, and kinesthetic aspects to help the students learn to identify tempo, respond to it, and use it musically, ultimately connecting the sound of it in different musical media.

LOTS were demonstrated through knowledge—that of saying the word *tempo* to describe fast and slow sounds—and comprehension, in that students could match the tempo of the teacher through singing and playing slowly and quickly. HOTS were evident at the point the students could apply their knowledge of tempo by demonstrating through performance without teacher modeling occurring at that moment. In other words, they could differentiate between slow and fast and perform without the teacher's cues.

Finally, the teacher made sure to recap the vocabulary and have the students demonstrate their understanding of tempo through lesson closure at the end of the class. This is an essential element, for we have no way of knowing if the students learned what we think we have taught them unless there is a way to assess them.

Because this was an initial lesson on tempo, *informal* assessment through verbalization of the vocabulary word, identification through body gestures for high and low sounds, and demonstration through the rows performing tempo are appropriate means of gathering data.

It would be prudent to use the informal assessment to drive the form of *formal* assessment implemented with subsequent lessons on tempo that would allow the teacher to determine how many of the students in the class can clap, read simple rhythmic patterns, and sing with different tempi; second, these data would assist the teacher in the planning and delivery of subsequent lessons until the concept had been fully mastered.

At that time, a more sophisticated set of lessons targeting tempo might be designed to further enhance the students' learning, such as teaching them the differences between adagio and allegro through hearing examples of the same piece performed at these tempi, then using a familiar song to have them perform at those tempi and to choose the appropriate one based on how effectively they can pronounce or read the words or play the beat accurately.

In essence, each level of lessons continues to build cognitive knowledge, physical acuity, and performance practices, creating a music repertoire for students. Furthermore, threaded lessons facilitate continued and consistent learning of that concept so that the learner has full command of it and can apply it in a variety of musical situations that include singing, performing, listening, moving, reading, and creating.

I will argue that threading each lesson is not a matter of throwing out the curriculum, but rather using those ideas that are already effective and organizing them so that they are integrated in threaded lessons. This is a matter of planning differently, not of necessarily eliminating or adding other elements. Thus, the mindset of the teacher is critical, for this manner of planning and delivering instruction is undoubtedly different from any training we have received, yet it includes all the musical elements that we already know. It is not new content; rather, it is forging new connections of that content.

Behavioral Threads

Because we teach children, it is necessary to have well-grounded and effective classroom management concepts associated with the curriculum. Most of us would probably agree that very little learning will be accomplished unless the students learn to function respectfully and responsively in the learning environment. In fact, I would argue that classroom management is the *first* element of instruction and that music learning follows it.

In establishing the learning environment, it behooves the teacher to create an inviting classroom that is interesting but not overly stimulative. The arrangement of the carpet, chairs, keyboard, sound system, instruments, and books is important. An orderly room sends a message that the teacher is prepared and organized and that he or she expects the same of his or her students.

Second, the teacher must be equipped with a formulated discipline policy complete with classroom guidelines for the students and the teacher to follow. He or she acts as the role model and does so through his or her attention to the students, responses to them, attitudes, caring manner, and follow-through with classroom learning experiences. Much of the communication we have is nonverbal and a number of studies have suggested that our messages can be conveyed nonverbally as much as 80 percent. Nonverbal communication has powerful potential to both turn on and turn off the learners.

Third, teachers teach students to be respectful by practicing respect in the way in which they handle their classrooms. The tone of the voice, the choice of verbiage, the volume of the voice, the eye contact, the time given to student questions and issues, and the perceived value of truth and honesty are communicated in everything the teacher says and does. The old adage "actions speak louder than words" appears to ring true.

Fourth, the concerted teaching of self-discipline is critical to an effective classroom. As teachers, we must instruct our students in taking responsibility for themselves and invest time and effort in teaching them to make good decisions. Fifth, we must have guidelines established that attend to procedures and activities. An excellent and practical source is a book by Wong and Wong (2005) called *The First Days of School*. It talks about the teacher's preparation before school begins and how he or she must anticipate all kinds of situations for which he or she must be ready. The authors make strong arguments for teaching students how to effectively function in the classroom so that the teacher has far fewer distractions with which to deal and can focus on content. Responsibility and self-monitoring are important elements to success in learning.

Sixth, the teacher must be ready to deliver quick-paced, interesting, and enactive lessons not only to increase learning, but also to avoid discipline problems. And seventh, the teacher must have a defined plan for dealing with classroom infractions in a consistent and fair manner.

I will maintain that there is no reason that students cannot cooperate and function as responsible learners as long as they are taught how to do so. If they are not cooperative and responsible, they are then likely to be a reflection of the teacher.

I learned a profound lesson one day when I was unexpectedly pulled into a third-grade math classroom. The teacher needed to get to the bathroom and I happened to be walking by her room. She begged me to take over class and I did so, only to find out that some of the students who were well behaved in my music classes were less so in math and a few who were sometimes troublesome for me displayed exemplary behavior in math.

As if a sudden bolt of lightening hit, I realized that they *choose* how they are behaving dependent on the expectations and/or situation. I was no longer going to allow them to make a choice that was less than excellent in my class! This changed the way I planned and delivered instruction and allowed my expectations to soar. The wonderful discovery was that the students always met my expectations—and these increased each year thereafter.

Students can do anything we want them to do as long as we teach them how to do it. They are smart, observant, and savvy. It is our job to capitalize on their abilities and allow them to be wonderful learners who contribute positively and cooperate fully in our classes. We must not accept less than wonderful things from them. Thus, I am concertedly integrating behavior into the lesson models so that there is a consistent reminder about expecting the best from the students.

Teaching good behavior is a matter of a three-pronged approach: explicitly stating your expectations, modeling what you want students to do so that they cannot misinterpret your directions, and providing verbal instruction in tandem with the modeling to ensure their understanding. Getting the best from them translates into more time to teach music content and enhanced learning for the students.

I will also suggest that the teacher who yells at the class will not resolve the issue. Rather, he or she will display his or her temper and will probably create more stress for the entire classroom while abusing his or her voice. In all my years of experience I have yet to see a teacher resolve an issue by yelling at the class. Second, the idea that a loud teacher begets a loud class seems to have some truth to it. It is possible that the teacher who talks over his or her students only teaches the class to talk louder and/or more frequently.

My rule of thumb is to talk softly so that the students have to "listen in." That took me a while to learn, but it works. I refuse to talk over them because I do not want to teach them that it is acceptable for them to talk when anyone else is talking to the class.

Teaching Students about Personal Space

From the very first day the music teacher meets his or her classes, it is imperative to establish expectations for both learning and for self-management. Students in music classes often engage in learning in which there might not be manipulatives with which to deal; thus they are sometimes tempted to let their hands and feet go wandering.

One of the most effective ways to teach students about personal space and self-management is use a hula hoop. I bring mine to class and demonstrate sitting inside it on the floor, modeling that my hands and feet are always inside of it and that I'm focusing on them just as they will focus on the learning. We practice using imaginary hula hoops during the kindergarten and first grade to establish those expectations. This helps them to understand that there are boundaries in the classroom. Thus, the concrete idea becomes abstract in a short while.

Focus of the Lessons

At the beginning of the year, it is efficient for the first few lessons to be teacher-centered until management is well established and the proper procedures have been taught to the classes for learning experiences that involve movement, getting and using instruments, and arriving at and departing from class. As the procedures are taught and rehearsed with the classes, the teacher can then begin to morph the focus into student-centered learning where the students are constantly engaged in active learning. The result of concerted rehearsal can eliminate confusion for the students and frustration for the teacher.

They Are Your Mirror!

Observations of many teachers have helped me to understand that children are basically good and they have the capability of choosing their behaviors and attitudes. A group of children can be wonderfully behaved and effective learners in one class and holy terrors in another. The variable is the teacher.

When I understood this, the words of one of my dearest friends, who left teaching and took a job in retail, came to life. She told me the two are essentially the same. It doesn't matter whether you are teaching children or selling hair products to salons. You have to make them want to buy the product whether or not they think they need it or like it. Her wisdom has guided me for many years.

We are essentially Sears Brand Central. We have to capture the students' interest, motivate them, attend to them, and sell learning. It's an amazing process and along the way there are no dull moments. To see them catch on to an idea or succeed with particular things such as matching pitch or creating their first improvisation is an incredible event. And with each success, they are much more likely to retain their motivation, participate in learning and risk-taking to attain that learning, and coach their peers. I cannot imagine another profession that allows us the opportunity to witness this.

Hedden's List for Success in the Classroom

There are several cardinal rules that I try to establish in preparing undergraduates for student teaching and the rigors of the job. These have proven to be most effective in guiding my own practice; thus I share them with teachers as signposts for the classroom. The teacher is advised to reflect on his or her own work and to consider existing research in order to effectively refine his or her own teaching. This is what I have learned so far:

1. Practice what you teach and preach. If your behavior counteracts your words, you will immediately lose credibility with

the students. Therefore, monitor your own words and actions. If you expect your students to listen quietly when someone is talking, practice the same behavior when dealing with parents or sitting in a faculty meeting.

2. Be ever-careful with your professional language, both in written and spoken form. I tabulate the number of times our undergraduates say such things as "OK," "you guys" (girls are not guys), "like," and "um" when teaching. They are often appalled to find that they've said "you guys" thirty times in a twenty-five–minute lesson or mumble "OK" after every learning segment. Talking "valley girl talk" with "like" every other "like" word in the "like" sentence is not "like" professional. The talk of the college student should become more professional as the student approaches student teaching.

3. Always model and verbalize your expectations for everything you teach. The children are learning everything, so you cannot assume they know how to do anything. That does not mean that you talk down to them or consider them stupid. It does mean that you teach them *everything* they need to know to successfully function in your classroom. And that includes how and when to sharpen a pencil, how to deal with getting a tissue, and how to handle entering and exiting the classroom. Nothing should be left for assumptions or you will have created a perfect place for a discipline problem to occur.

4. Be consistent in establishing starting pitch and tempo cues (in the correct meter!) every time the students sing or perform. They will learn to anticipate this and can eventually do it for themselves, but that requires concerted, consistent attention.

5. For every element of the lesson, prepare them for success by briefly explaining what they'll be learning, modeling expectations, and rehearsing with the class. The critical element to remember is never to make assumptions about what they know. It's our job to teach them everything they need to know to succeed in our classrooms.

6. Never put yourself in a situation where you argue with a student or lose your temper. Getting angry never resolves an issue. Be mindful that your job is that of a problem-solver, both musically and behaviorally. I will reiterate that there is no reason the students cannot be effective learners and responsible, well-behaved class members, but all of this depends on *you*. You establish the rules and set the tone. You communicate expectations and repair anything that was not accomplished.

7. Watch and listen! Students are constantly providing nonverbal information to you, so do not ignore it. I often laugh about this, but feel that my many years of teaching general music allowed me to learn about body language, so much so that I could often anticipate someone had to go to the restroom before he or she realized it. Body language is quite telling, so pay attention to it.

8. Remember that you are a public employee and your behavior both inside and outside of school is on display. You only get one reputation, so be careful to protect it. Make good decisions for yourself so that you model that for children. In one of my schools, a high school teacher often would over-imbibe every Saturday night and stand in the middle of downtown to be a traffic cop. The students would drive through downtown around midnight just to laugh at him. They often commented about lack of respect for him because of the way he mishandled himself.

9. Remember to politely *tell* your students to do things such as stand up, line up at the door, and take their books out quietly rather than *ask* them. If you ask a question, you might not like the results. You've given them the opportunity to say "no." Tell, don't ask.

10. Treat your students as you would want to be treated. They will maintain their interest in music if you are inviting, considerate, competent, prepared, have high expectations, and make learning worthwhile and enjoyable.

11. Remember that you are teaching classroom management that includes self-management and positive behavior first, music

content second, social learning third, and a variety of necessary skills fourth (e.g., tying shoes, zipping coats, and handling things such as restroom trips and the drinking fountain).

12. Even though you may be the only music teacher in your building, there are many other teachers who can be highly effective mentors. Teaching is teaching. Those skills that contribute to good teaching in one area transfer to another such as from science to social studies to music; only the content changes. Methodology, pedagogy, expectations, classroom management, and the like are present in every classroom (the degrees of which are highly variable depending on the teacher).

13. As a teacher, you work with people. It's all about the people—students, colleagues, parents, administration, and the community. You must make every effort to remember that you are teaching *people* music rather than teaching music. Make every effort to hone your human relations skills, for the school and the community will not respond well to the diva mentality. Leave that one on the stage after you finish your senior recital.

CHAPTER FOUR

MODELS OF THREADED LESSONS

•

T he following learning experiences are designed to demonstrate how to plan lesson instruction based on one concept for each lesson. The reader is cautioned that the lessons are designed to be templates for planning and delivering instruction and do not necessarily encompass a vast range of music genres or periods of music. The lessons are quite specific in terms of verbiage to introduce, teach, and provide feedback to the learners. The reader will also notice that classroom management is built into the lessons through particular expectations communicated by the teacher.

The reader is strongly encouraged to ensure that each group of students is taught how to undertake each aspect of the classroom, ranging from getting textbooks to handling instruments to handling themselves. This requires attention to modeling, clearly communicating expectations, and then rehearsing those expectations with the students before assuming they know what to do.

Each lesson exists as its own entity and by no means constitutes a curriculum. The models demonstrate how to plan instruction based on the threading idea, so that one concept serves as the basis for a lesson that includes a variety of learning experiences to teach and reinforce that concept.

The following lessons are templates for introducing particular concepts through threaded musical experiences. You will notice that there is repetition of the vocabulary and it appears in tandem with each element of the lesson. Every segment of the lesson bleeds into the next so that the concept is never confused with any other. Furthermore, behavior is also threaded throughout the experiences so that the teacher can simultaneously shape the behavior while communicating expectations through modeling and verbal directives.

The most important elements of the lesson are that the children are enactively making music, engaged in singing, moving, listening, performing, creating, and reading with closure that recaps their learning for the day. Both lower-order and higher-order thinking skills are achieved in the lessons, allowing the students to use their knowledge and skills in different ways. Notice that the models utilize all of these components and are designed to meet the needs of visual, aural, and kinesthetic learners.

Be aware that some of the first lessons present the ideas of the content without much verbal inclusion from the teacher; the other lessons, however, are more specific to the verbal instruction. The intent is to demonstrate both sequence and verbiage through different lessons.

References to the National Standards in the lesson models are from the *National Standards for Arts Education: What Every Young American Should Know and Be Able to Do in the Arts*, by the Consortium of National Arts Education Associations (Reston, VA: MENC, 1994).

Lesson Models

The Lesson Model: Grade K

Concept: *Steady beat*, threaded through every segment of this lesson
National Standards:

1. Singing, alone and with others, a varied repertoire of music.

2. Performing on instruments, alone and with others, a varied repertoire of music.

3. Improvising melodies, variations, and accompaniments.

4. Reading and notating music.

5. Listening to, analyzing, and describing music.

Introduction (Visual, Auditory, and Kinesthetic)
Materials:

- The "Are You Sleeping?" song for teacher

Procedure:

1. "Today we're going to explore things that make a sound that you hear again and again. I'm going to clap a sound [teacher claps four quarter notes, designated as 1111] and you'll probably notice that the sound happens more than once. Let me clap this again and I'll have you count how many times it happens [1111], but don't blurt it out loud, only show me with your fingers [behavior]."

2. "Now I'm going to do a different number and this time just THINK the number in your head without blurting it out loud. I'll ask one person to tell me when we're done thinking [11111111]. Please quietly raise your hand if you know the answer and I'll ask Brian to tell me how many he heard. If you agree that this is the right number, please nod your head 'yes.' If you do not agree, please shake your head 'no' [behavior]. Let's check it. I'll clap it again and you count out loud [11111111]. Yes, it is eight times."

3. "I'm going to clap this again and tell you that we call this a steady beat [teacher demonstrates]. Please clap it with me [they do it together]. Now let's add a song we know well and keep clapping a steady beat to 'Are You Sleeping?' [traditional song]." The teacher initiates the beat, sings a starting pitch cue for the class, and the class joins in song.

Moving (Auditory and Kinesthetic)
Materials:

- Guitar, recorder, or hand drum

Procedure:

1. The teacher uses a guitar, recorder, or hand drum and instructs the children that they will be following him or her around a circle with their feet. The rules are simple: They cannot touch anybody or anything (if they do, the teacher will have them sit

down immediately, then restate the rules and rehearse them with the class again, doing this until they respond correctly).

2. Teacher moves students into a large circle and shows them how to turn a quarter turn to walk the circle, modeling what is expected and speaking the directives (behavior).

3. Teacher uses the guitar, recorder, or hand drum to play steady beats and walks with the children, speaking "walk, walk, walk, walk" until they are in sync. He or she then has them stop, freeze, and asks them to walk in place to the steady beat as he or she plays another round of steady beats. The children sit down on the floor as he or she moves to the next step of the lesson.

Singing (Auditory and Kinesthetic)
Materials:

- The "A, B, C" song for the teacher

Procedure:

1. "We have a new song to learn today and you'll hear the steady beat as I patsch this on my legs during the song." Teacher sings both lines of "A, B, C" (traditional song) and patsches. Next, he or she asks the class to patsch with him or her as he or she sings the song again. The third time, he or she asks them to play gently as he or she sings it softly.

2. Now that they have heard it three times, he or she sings a phrase and asks the class to echo; he or she proceeds through the two phrases and then they all sing the whole song. Gently, patsching is added as they sing it softly. Then they continue the steady beat with a medium dynamic of singing. The teacher then asks them to clap the steady beat as they sing.

3. Finally, teacher asks students to patsch the steady beat while they sing the song in their heads as he or she mouths the words to keep them together. The teacher reinforces the concept, telling the class that they played the steady beat on their bodies with the song, but are now going to read it and play it on instruments.

Reading and Writing (Visual and Kinesthetic)
    Materials:

- Chart with red hearts iconically representing beat

- Toy stethoscope

- Music stand

Procedure:

1. The teacher shows the class an iconic representation of steady beat with a chart of red hearts (four or eight can be repeated easily). He or she points to the hearts and tells the class these are beats just like their heartbeats, but they can *see* these and they can't see their own heartbeats without special equipment.

2. Teacher has a toy stethoscope and the class hears the heartbeat of one child and they clap the beat. The teacher uses the icons, pointing to each one as the class claps the steady beat. He or she says that they are *reading* the beats. The class is instructed to clap the beats as he or she sings "A, B, C," and the teacher points to the icons as he or she sings and they clap. Next, the teacher asks the class to sing the song and clap the steady beat as he or she points to the icons.

3. Now that the class can clap the beats together, they are ready for instruments. The teacher props the icon chart on a music stand and gives instructions for the instruments (behavior).

Performing (Visual, Auditory, and Kinesthetic)
    Materials:

- Unpitched percussion instruments (shakers, hand drums, and sand blocks) for the class

Procedure:

1. "Boys and girls, we are going to play steady beat on our instruments today. In a minute you will have either a shaker [teacher demonstrates steady beat on the shaker], a hand drum [demonstrates], or sand blocks [demonstrates]. Your job is to handle

these carefully so that they do not break and to play the steady beat *with our song*. Let me show you how you will get these."

2. The teacher walks to the shaker, picks it up, and silently carries it back to his or her place, telling the class that the instrument is for playing music, but it must remain quiet until everyone is ready to play. The teacher sets the instrument on the floor in front of him- or herself and lets it rest. He or she does this with the hand drum and the sand blocks, then allows a group of students to get their instruments.

3. Teacher mentions that Bill is carrying his sand blocks very quietly and thanks him for following directions and that Amanda is waiting patiently with her hand drum on the floor (behavior reinforcement). Another group gets their instruments and he or she does the same thing, noticing good behavior and commenting on it. Finally, the last group gets theirs.

4. When everyone is ready, they all pick up their instruments and practice steady beat with the teacher clapping to lead them. He or she then uses the icon, pointing to the beats, and the class plays along.

5. Next, the teacher adds the song and they play and sing with him or her. The teacher asks them to play medium loud and sing with it, then to sing softly and play gently with it (we are winding down and want less sound). Then he or she asks them to rest their instruments in their laps.

6. The teacher models how to return the instrument to the shelf and has each group do so without noise, again noticing who handles it as directed and giving overt feedback to those students (behavior reinforcement). He or she reinforces the vocabulary by telling them that they played steady beat on their instruments.

Improvising, Composing, and Creating (Visual, Auditory, and Kinesthetic)
Materials: None

Procedure:

1. The teacher asks the class to raise their hands if they know of other things that have a steady beat besides their hearts and he or she will ask a few students for examples. The teacher may

need to prompt them with an idea or two such as windshield washers, a ticking clock, or a panting dog.

2. Teacher asks one student to use his or her body to make a steady beat like a windshield washer and has the class mimic it; then they do this with other ideas that the children provide.

Listening (Visual, Auditory, and Kinesthetic)
Materials:

- Recording of "Stars and Stripes Forever"

- Picture of John Philip Sousa

Procedure:

1. The teacher tells the class that he or she has a fun piece of music for them to hear and that they will try to find the steady beat of the song after they listen to a bit of it. He or she instructs then to prepare for listening by opening their ears, resting their lips, and letting their hands rest in their laps (teacher models this).

2. Teacher shows a picture of Sousa and shares that Sousa liked to write music for bands to play. The teacher plays the first section of a recording of Sousa's "Stars and Stripes Forever" (written in 1896) as they listen, then leads them in finding the beat with gentle patching on their legs as it is played again (forty-five to sixty seconds of the piece).

Closure and Check of Learning (Visual, Auditory, and Kinesthetic)
"Today we learned about sounds that sound alike."

- Identification: Teacher asks a student to point to a beat on the chart (icon).

- Verbalization: Teacher asks the class to blurt (concerted attention to getting a group response) the new thing they learned today (steady beat).

- Demonstration: Teacher plays steady beat on the guitar, recorder, or drum and has the class demonstrate that they can clap steady beat.

- Further application: Teacher asks students to find something that makes steady beat and tell class about it in the next music class (to maintain the focus on the concept, expect account-ability, and connect to subsequent lessons).

LOTS

Echoing the teacher with clapping, patsching, walking, reading, and performing of steady beat.

HOTS

Identifying other things that possess steady beat and demonstrating the concept with their bodies, creating a new application of steady beat.

The Lesson Model: Grade K

Concept: *Melody, specifically high and low sounds*, threaded through every segment of this lesson

National Standards:

1. Singing, alone and with others, a varied repertoire of music.

2. Performing on instruments, alone and with others, a varied repertoire of music.

3. Improvising melodies, variations, and accompaniments.

4. Reading and notating music.

5. Listening to, analyzing, and describing music.

Introduction (Auditory and Visual)
Materials:

- Ball

Procedure:

1. "Boys and girls, today we are going to learn about different sounds. I have a ball and I'm going to throw it up high. Please

watch it with your eyes [teacher tosses it up]. Now I'm going to bounce it on the floor, so I'm going to throw it low. Please watch this with your eyes [teachers bounces it on the floor]."

2. "We're going to make some sounds to have our voices follow the ball. Watch this. If I throw the ball high, I'm going to use my voice to go up high [teacher demonstrates on a particular sound such as 'ah' or 'loo']. Now you try it with me [he or she throws the ball up high and the class follows it with their voices]."

3. When they have successfully made high sounds, proceed in the same manner with low sounds. After that, the vocabulary is introduced: "What we just did was to make high and low sounds. When we sing, our songs have high and low sounds. I'm going to move to the piano and show you more of these."

Listening (Auditory, Visual, and Kinesthetic)
Materials:

• Piano or keyboard

Procedure:

1. The teacher goes to the piano to physically and aurally demonstrate high and low sounds. "Rest your hands in your lap and just use your ears for this. If I stand here, I can play very high sounds [he or she plays snippets of a couple of familiar songs]. If I stand at the other end of the piano, I can play very low sounds." He or she plays bits of familiar songs.

2. "Let's practice these. If I move back up to the other end of the piano and play a high sound [plays an example], please indicate that with a 'thumbs up' [teacher demonstrates]." The teacher does two different examples on very high pitches. "If I move back to the other end of the piano and play low sounds like this [he or she demonstrates], you will give me a 'thumbs down.' Let's practice this."

3. The teacher exaggerates moving from the high end to the low end and plays a couple of examples at each end, offering specific

feedback about their responses, such as "You were exactly right about those sounds being high ones," or "Absolutely correct, 'thumbs down' on the low sounds." When a few examples of each have been practiced, the teacher segues to movement.

Moving (Auditory, Visual, and Kinesthetic)
Materials:

- Piano or keyboard

Procedure:

1. "Now that you can *hear* the difference between high and low sounds, watch me as I show a high sound with my body." The teacher stretches up high to show one way to indicate a high sound, then raises his or her hand to indicate another way, all done while verbalizing respective high sounds. He or she asks the class to try one with him or her and plays a high sound, modeling the body response to that sound.

2. The teacher then moves to the opposite end of the piano and repeats this rehearsal, showing the children how his or her body could bend down to the ground, slump over, or move the hand toward his or her feet to show the sound is low. The teacher and the class practice indicating a low sound with their bodies. "You showed high and low sounds with your bodies. I can see and hear the difference."

Singing, Reading, and Writing (Auditory, Visual, and Kinesthetic)
Materials:

- Iconic chart with stars to represent pitches
- The "Twinkle, Twinkle, Little Star" song for the teacher

Procedure:

1. Using the song "Twinkle, Twinkle, Little Star" (traditional song), the teacher can show the direction of the melody with

an iconic chart of stars placed at the different pitch levels. The teacher asks the class to listen and watch as he or she points to the stars to show high and low sounds.

2. After showing this, he or she asks the children to use an "invisible marker" to trace the melody in the air as he or she sings the song to them.

3. Finally, he or she asks them to sing it and trace it again, but also to notice a high sound. The teacher asks the students to raise their hands if they could point to the highest sound on the chart, and asks one student to go the chart and point to a high sound, reinforcing the correct response. Teacher has the class sing the song again as he or she points to the stars and slowly emphasizes the high pitches.

4. "You noticed the high sounds. Let's see if we can find the low sounds this time." Teacher repeats the process by asking the class to listen and watch as he or she sings the song to find the lowest sound. Again, the class traces the contour in the air.

5. The teacher asks a student to point to the lowest sound and the class sings as the teacher points to each pitch (star). "You now can *hear* and *see* high and low sounds. Excellent job finding the differences between the high and low sounds, boys and girls. We're going to play those on our instruments today."

Performing (Auditory, Visual, and Kinesthetic)
Materials:

- Barred instruments with only low and high Gs in place (xylophones, metallophones, and glockenspiels)

- Appropriate mallets, one per student

- The "Twinkle, Twinkle, Little Star" song for the teacher

Procedure:

1. In preparation for this, barred instruments—xylophones, metallophones, and glockenspiels—are used with only the low G

and high G (the common notes found in the C and G7 chords for this song). The teacher does not give the students mallets until later.

2.   He or she demonstrates how to stand up, walk over to the instruments, and sit down, and then shows the class how to touch the *big* G bar in its center, noting it makes low sounds. He or she uses the mallet to play the low G and sings a bit of the song with that bar; he or she then touches and plays the *little* G bar and tells them they'll be using it to play the high sounds.

3.   The teacher asks one student to show the class how to walk to the instruments, sit down behind one, and wait patiently for everyone else. Next, a row of students is asked to follow what the model did.

4.   When everyone is seated behind the instruments, the class is instructed to touch the low G in the middle of the bar while the teacher sings that pitch and then repeats this with high G. The teacher shows the class how to hold the mallet to strike the bar's center (one per student to optimize motor skills), and distributes the mallets.

5.   The students play low G together as the teacher pulses the beat with his or her hand. The teacher then instructs them to continue to play that note as he or she sings "Twinkle, Twinkle."

6.   Upon finishing, he or she asks the class to blurt out the answer to this question: "Did you play a high sound or a low sound?" If there is confusion, he or she plays low G and than high G and asks the class to again play their note. "Was it a high G or a low G?" The teacher does not spoonfeed the answer, but rather lets them come to the correct conclusion.

   Next, he or she does the same thing with high G and asks the same question to the class. If they have distinguished correctly between low G and high G, the teacher proceeds; if not, he or she will need to play and sing the low and high pitches and allow the students time to practice listening and identifying until they can correctly do so (this might take a minute or two of rehearsal during more than one class to accomplish).

Improvising, Composing, and Creating (Auditory and Kinesthetic)
Materials:

- The "London Bridge Is Falling Down" song for the teacher

Procedure:

1. An older, familiar song is used, with the teacher leading the singing and reviewing of "London Bridge Is Falling Down" (traditional singing game). "It's your turn to try making your own music on the instruments. Please find a low sound that you can play while I sing the song." The class is asked to find a low sound on their instruments to play (again using the Gs common to the two chords in the song) during the song; the teacher claps a steady beat, cues them to begin, and provides a large cut-off.

2. This is repeated with high sounds. If the teacher strongly establishes the beat, the students will most likely play with the beat; however, attention to rhythm is not important, for the focus is only on high and low responses.

Closure and Check of Learning

"Today we learned about two different kinds of sounds. Let's see what you know about these."

- Identification: Teacher asks a student to point to a high sound (icon) on the chart for "Twinkle, Twinkle," then another student to indicate a low sound.

- Verbalization: Teacher asks the class to make a high sound with their voices, then a low one while he or she points to the corresponding icon.

- Demonstration: Teacher plays a low sound and asks the class to show him or her if it is a low sound with a "thumbs down" or a high sound with a "thumbs up."

- Further application: Teacher asks the students to find something that makes a low sound or a high sound at home or outside and tell the class about it in the next music class (to maintain the focus on the concept and expect accountability).

LOTS

Singing the songs as a group, performing low and high Gs on their instruments, and using movement to rehearse responses to high and low sounds.

HOTS

Analyzing the sounds and responding physically (with thumbs up or down and with performance on the instruments) and verbally to the respective sounds.

The Lesson Model: Grade K

Concept: *As a precursor to form, the lesson introduces patterns*, threaded through every segment of this lesson

National Standards:

1. Singing, alone and with others, a varied repertoire of music.

2. Performing on instruments, alone and with others, a varied repertoire of music.

3. Improvising melodies, variations, and accompaniments.

4. Reading and notating music.

5. Listening to, analyzing, and describing music.

Introduction (Auditory and Visual)

Materials:

- Icons of large red and blue circles

- Two identical pictures of redheaded children

Procedure:

1. "Boys and girls, today I will ask you to pretend to be a music teacher and see if you can discover something about what I'm doing. I have two red circles that I'm going to put on the board and then there is a blue one. I have two more red circles and another blue one. Oh, my, there are two more red circles and

another blue one." The teacher puts the circles in a row, making three rows of the red-red-blue pattern.

2. "If you notice something about these, please put your hand on your knee. I will ask one person to tell me what you're noticing." There may be a variety of responses, but the word *pattern* might emerge. If it does not, the teacher must validate the fact that the children have responded and then tell them, "I have made a pattern. Now let's see if we can make one together."

3. "This time I'm going to use your hair color. Brian, you have brown hair. Would you please stand next to me? I have blonde hair and Brian has brown hair. Touch your head if you know how to make another pattern like Brian's and mine. How would you make one?" The teacher lets the children give their responses, ultimately guiding them to suggest the correct ones. The pattern will be visible and they will be able to determine if it is correct or not.

4. When there are three repetitions of blonde-brown, the teacher follows with "Yes, you made a new pattern that goes blonde-brown, blonde-brown, blonde-brown. I'm so glad you can see how to make a pattern. Let's see if we can count how many times our blonde-brown pattern occurs." The teacher touches his or her head and counts "one," then touches the heads to count patterns "two" and "three." "We made the pattern happen three times."

5. "I'm going to put a *different* pattern in between pattern two and three. Watch this." The teacher has pictures of two red-headed children and places them on the floor between the standing children in the patterns. "Please nod your head 'yes' if you think the new pattern is the same as the blonde-brown pattern—or shake your head 'no' if you think the new pattern is different from the blonde-brown patterns."

6. If students respond "yes," the teacher will have to retouch the heads, speaking "blonde, brown" and reteaching the pattern. If they respond "no," the teacher says, "You are exactly correct. You are seeing a different pattern. So now we have the blonde-brown pattern with Brian and me; next we have the

same pattern with Roger and Nicole; a *different* pattern with the redheaded pictures; and then the *same* pattern with Jenna and Joel."

7. "Thank you for being our patterns. You may sit down. Now we're going to do a pattern with our feet. Without touching anybody and without any noise, watch me walk over to the carpet area and start a circle." The teacher models this and then asks one child to show the class how to do this. When the child has done this well, the teacher compliments the model and asks several students to do the same; he or she proceeds until all children are in the circle and then compliments the class on following directions.

8. If they do not do this as asked, the teacher will need to re-model it and start over, rehearsing this until they can successfully do it. It is important not to reinforce behavior that is not what you modeled and expected, so do not hesitate to practice with them until they do it as you asked.

Moving (Visual, Auditory, and Kinesthetic)
Materials:

- Woodblock and mallet

Procedure:

1. "Now that you are standing in a circle, let me show you about our patterns. When I play the woodblock with walking notes [quarter notes], you are going to walk around the circle like this [teacher models]; when I play the woodblock with running notes [eighth notes], you are going to carefully jog around the circle like this." The teacher models.

2. "Let's practice walking notes. Rea-dy, and here we go." Teacher plays the woodblock and they walk with several walking notes. "You did those beautifully, walking right with my woodblock. Now let's try the gentle running notes. Listen to them go faster [he or she models]. When we run gently, we

do not get to touch anybody else or anything. We want to use only good manners." The teacher would need to have a "perpetrator" sit this one out.

3. The teacher plays several running notes and then instructs the class to do it with him or her. "Your ears are working well. I saw you running gently and you knew to do these differently from the walking notes. Because you know walking notes and running notes, I'm going to play some of each. Please make your feet go with the sound of the woodblock as I play them." The teacher plays three walking notes and then announces that the pattern repeats.

4. "This time there are six walking notes. Listen to that pattern [the teacher plays it]. Now a change is going to occur. The running notes are next. Listen as I play eight running notes [the teacher plays it]. And at the end, there are three walking notes [the teacher plays it]." This sequence aligns with the rhythm of the words in the song, so the preparation with attention to detail is important.

5. "Please sit down right where your feet are. I'm going to ask you to be the teacher again and tell me about the pattern we just did. Let me show you the walking notes [teacher demonstrates]. If I do running notes [teacher demonstrates], are these the same or different from the walking notes? [If the answer is not correct, the teacher will need to guide them to the correct response by demonstrating again.] If I go back to walking notes, are these the same as the running notes? [Teacher demonstrates both.]"

6. "I just made a pattern. Let me show you all of these notes. When I'm done, please keep the pattern a secret until I ask one person to tell me what it is." The teacher demonstrates the six walking, eight running, and three walking notes and asks a student to identify the pattern (the child will say "walking" and "running" to distinguish the notes).

7. "Nice work, teachers. You figured out that we have walking, then running, and more walking notes in our pattern. We are

now going to learn to read these. Watch as I show you what they look like."

Reading and Writing (Kinesthetic and Visual)
Materials:

- Whiteboard, marker, and eraser

Procedure:

1. The teacher asks the children to face their bodies toward the board and then draws one walking (quarter) note on the white-board. "When we see the walking note, it means we can clap it one time [he or she demonstrates]. Or we could sing it [he or she demonstrates singing it on *la*]. Or we could play it on an instrument [he or she demonstrates playing it on the woodblock]. It means music. This is how we write and read music."

2. "Please play this walking note with me by clapping it once. Rea-dy, and here we clap. [The class claps one quarter note.] Now I'm going to write the first part of our pattern. [Teacher writes three quarter notes on the board.] Please clap these as I point to them. Rea-dy, and here we clap. [The class claps these.] The pattern is now repeated, so there are six walking notes. Play with me. Rea-dy, and here we clap [the class claps these]. You just learned to read walking notes!"

3. "Now we'll see what running notes look like. [The teacher draws four sets of eighth notes on the board.] Watch and listen as I point to these with one hand and tap my leg with the other hand to play them [he or she demonstrates]. It's your turn to clap the running notes. Rea-dy, and here we clap. [The class claps the eight eighth notes.]"

4. "You've clapped the running notes and the walking notes, but now I'm wondering if you can switch back to walking notes to clap these three walking notes. [Teacher writes three quarter notes.] Rea-dy, and here we clap. [The class claps the three quarter notes.] Wow, you did it perfectly!"

5. "I think you're ready to clap the six walking notes [teacher points to these], the eight running notes [points to these], and the three walking notes [points] without stopping. Rea-dy, and here we clap. [The class claps the rhythm.] My gosh, you've learned how to read music! That was done with perfect changes between the walking and running notes. You are now ready to read those notes in our song."

Singing (Visual and Auditory)
Materials:

- Poster of the "Hot Cross Buns" song with pitch levels noted

Procedure:

1. The teacher has a large poster of "Hot Cross Buns" (traditional song) with the notes written on the poster at pitch levels but without the staff. Since there are three pitches, one is placed higher, one is in the middle, and one is lower. These are easy for kindergarteners to distinguish as being up/down or same/different. The teacher covers up everything except for the first pattern (three quarter notes).

2. "Look at my pattern. Please clap this with me. Rea-dy, and here we clap [the class claps it]. You remembered how to clap that! Good for you. Now look at the next pattern [he or she uncovers the next three quarter notes]. If you think it looks like the first pattern, give me a 'thumbs up' [teacher models a 'thumbs up']; if you think it looks different, give me a 'thumbs down' [teacher models a 'thumbs down']."

3. If the class responds correctly, the teacher can move on. If not, he or she must have them clap the first pattern, then the second one before re-asking the question. Assuming the response is correct, he or she says, "You clapped the walking notes perfectly. Let's look at the next pattern [the teacher uncovers the four eighth-note pairs]. If it looks like the other pattern, nod your head 'yes'; if it looks different, shake your head 'no.' You are correct again; this one is different."

4. "Here's the last pattern [the teacher uncovers it]. If you think it looks like another pattern, raise your hand and I'll ask one person to show us which pattern it is like. [The teacher has one child go to the board and point to the quarter note pattern at the beginning of the song.] Yes, you did it."

5. "Hmmm. I see three walking notes at the beginning [he or she points to them], another three walking notes [he or she points to the next three notes], and then three more at the end [points]. But in the middle is another pattern [points]. If this is *different* than the other pattern, please wave to me [the children wave]. You are correct again. These are our running notes."

6. "Listen to me sing the song as you read the walking and running notes. [The teacher sings 'Hot Cross Buns' as he or she points to each note, showing the class that reading occurs from left to right, but not saying that yet; that comes later.] What we have is a same–same–different–same pattern." He or she points to show these.

7. "Let me sing the *same* pattern to you and then you sing back to me. Please sit up tall and get your best singing voices ready. [The teacher sings 'hot cross buns' and the class echoes him or her.] Here is another *same* pattern [he or she sings the second *same* pattern]."

8. "Here's the *different* pattern [he or she sings 'one a penny, two a penny' and the class echoes]. And here's the *same* pattern again [he or she sings 'hot cross buns']."

9. "Please listen to the whole song and read it as I point to the notes. [The teacher points to each note and sings the song.] It's your turn. I'll point and you read and sing it." He or she sings the starting pitch on "one, rea-dy, sing" and the class sings.

10. "Let's sing it softly this time. I'll point and you read and sing it. One, rea-dy, sing. [The class sings it softly.] Now let's sing it a bit louder—not yelling—but a little louder. One, rea-dy, sing. [The class sings.]"

11. "Let's do it a little faster this time. One, rea-dy, sing. [The class sings again.] I think you're very good at reading this

song! In a moment you are going to get percussion instruments. I bet you remember that we usually strike these to play them and that you will handle them with care."

Performing (Visual and Kinesthetic)
Materials:

- Poster of the song

- Unpitched percussion instruments (enough for the class)

Procedure:

1. The teacher shows the class how to retrieve the instruments, saying, "Watch me walk over to the percussion instruments without touching anybody or anything. I will get an instrument, carry it back to my place without making noise, and then put it on the floor so I can wait patiently until it's time to play. John, please show the class how to do this. [John demonstrates.] You did exactly what I asked. Thank you."

2. "While John is waiting patiently, these seven students [the teacher makes eye contact with them to establish the directive] may quietly and carefully get an instrument. Everyone, watch as they do what John did. He is still waiting patiently for us. Now, the next seven students will do that. Thank you for waiting patiently. I love it when you handle this so well—and the next seven students will get their instruments quietly and carefully. I am impressed that you listened so well and handled the instruments so carefully. Thank you."

3. "Please get ready to play our song while I point to the notes. One, rea-dy, play. [The teacher points to the notes as the class plays, giving them a huge cut-off at the end.] You finished right with me. Thank you for watching so carefully. Let's play it again and be even gentler this time. One, rea-dy, play. [The teacher models this gently with an instrument.] You did it gently, as I asked. Thank you. Let's play it a tad faster this time. Listen to me speed it up just a little bit [he or she demonstrates]."

4. "Read it while I point to the notes. One, rea-dy, play [the class plays it]. Now you are ready to play the patterns. The girls will play the *same* pattern [he or she points to those on the board] and the boys will play the *different* pattern [points]. [The class plays this and then the teacher switches the parts.] You listened and read that well. Thank you for reading music today. We are going to play a different pattern, so get ready for a change."

Improvising, Composing, Creating, and Listening (Kinesthetic and Visual)
Materials:

- Unpitched percussion instruments

Procedure:

1. "Sara, please play a short pattern on your tambourine and I'll play a *different* one back to you. [Sara plays, then the teacher plays, making the last pattern obviously different from Sara's.] Greg, play a new pattern and then I'll play a different one. [The teacher repeats the procedure.]"

2. "Everyone, get your instrument ready and I'll point to you when it's your turn to play a pattern. I'll play a different one back to you." The teacher lets each child play a short pattern as he or she moves by each student to *respond* with proximity, eye contact, and a nonverbal message that lets each child know the teacher is listening.

Closure and Check of Learning
"Today we learned about patterns. I'm so curious to see what you know about these."

- Identification: Teacher asks a student to point to a same pattern in the song and another to point to a *different* pattern in the song.

- Verbalization: Teacher asks the class to sing the *same* pattern (there are three) after giving them the starting pitch cue, "one, rea-dy, sing."

- Demonstration: Teacher asks the class to clap the *different* pattern while they sing the words in their heads, giving them a counting cue, "one, rea-dy, clap."

- Further application: Teacher asks the students to find something that has a pattern at home or outside and tell the class about it in the next music class (to maintain the focus on the concept and expect accountability).

LOTS

Singing the songs as a group, performing the walking and running notes on instruments, and physically indicating *same* and *different* with their bodies.

HOTS

Analyzing the patterns to determine *same* and *different*, reading the notes, and creating new patterns on their instruments.

The Lesson Model: Grade K

Concept: *Solo versus group, as a precursor to harmony*, threaded through every segment of this lesson
National Standards:

1. Singing, alone and with others, a varied repertoire of music.

2. Performing on instruments, alone and with others, a varied repertoire of music.

3. Improvising melodies, variations, and accompaniments.

4. Reading and notating music.

5. Listening to, analyzing, and describing music.

Introduction (Auditory)
Materials:

- The "Jingle Bells" song for the teacher

Procedure:

1. "Boys and girls, today I have a new word for you. It's called *solo* and it means one person singing alone. If I sing 'Jingle Bells' [Pierpont, written in 1857] to you with just my own voice, I'm singing a solo. Let me show you." The teacher models the chorus of the song.

Singing (Auditory)
Materials:

- The "Jingle Bells" song for the teacher

Procedure:

1. "We're going to learn that song today. First, I'll sing a little bit to you as a solo and you'll sing it back with everyone in the group." The teacher proceeds to sing short phrases to the class, carefully establishing the starting pitch for the class to echo, and then proceeds with singing longer chunks (each two phrases in length), after which the class echoes.

2. "I'm going to sing the song again. When you hear me begin my solo, please wave at me. [The teacher starts the song and checks to ensure that the class is giving the signal.] Now let's change this. You get to sing this as a *group*, so there won't be just one solo. [The teacher provides the starting pitch and cue and lets them sing together.] You sang together as a group and remembered the song."

3. "Let's see if we can learn a little bit more about solos and groups. In a minute we will be in a circle on the rug and we'll be using our bodies to do things as solos and groups."

Moving (Visual and Kinesthetic)
Materials:

- Hula hoop

Procedure:

1. "Watch me as I walk over to the carpet. I'm walking as a *solo*, not touching anybody or anything. Angela, would you please do a solo walk to the carpet and start a circle for us? [Teacher waits for her to do this.] Brad, Suzanne, and Terry, please walk as a *group* and join our circle . . . Billy, walk over as a solo . . . and everyone else walk over as a group."

2. When everyone is in place the teacher begins careful instruction to set boundaries. "I have a hula hoop that I'm going to use [he or she sets it on the floor and steps into it]. This is my personal space. My whole body has to stay inside my hula hoop. Please pretend that you have an imaginary hula hoop. Hold yours around your waist like mine . . . and then lay it on the floor . . . and step inside it. Your bodies must stay inside your hoop. Now please sit down inside your imaginary hoop."

3. "I'm going to stand up and show you one way I could move my body as a *solo* inside my hoop. Please watch me. [Teacher demonstrates stretching his or her hands up high and down low, moving his or her hips from side to side, and standing tall and squatting.] Please stand up inside your hoops and practice your own solo in your own hoop while I count to ten. One, two . . . ten."

4. The teacher monitors this and then gives a physical cut-off. "Thank you for practicing that. Please sit down in your hoops. I will ask one person to show me a solo and we'll all watch that body solo. Aidan, please stand up and show us your solo. Everyone, put your eyes on Aidan and be a good audience while we watch his solo. [The teacher cuts this off after a few seconds.] Thank you, Aidan. Sally, please show us your solo. Everyone, put your eyes on Sally and be a good audience. . . . Thank you, Sally."

5. "Now let's see if we can do one movement as a *group*. Please stand up inside your hoops and do what I do. Our group will be moving the same way all together. [The teacher again stretches up high, bends over to touch the ground, moves his or her hips

from side to side, stands tall, and squats.] That time we moved as a group and that's different from your solos."

6. "Please do your own solo while I count to five and then we'll do our group movement. Rea-dy and go! One, two, three, four, five. Freeze. Now let's change and do the same thing together as a group."

7. "Follow me. [Teacher walks in place inside the hoop, jumps up and down, and then rubs his or her tummy while the class mirrors.] Freeze. Change back to your solos while I count to five. One, two, three, four, five. Freeze. Let's move as a group again. [Teacher leads them in moving his or her elbows to flap like a chicken, wiggling his or her nose, and moving his or her head up and down.] Freeze."

8. "You watched very closely and did the same thing as I did in our group. Please sit down inside your hoop. We are going to use only our ears for the next part. You will hear a solo and a group. [As the teacher moves to the keyboard, he or she instructs the class to face him or her inside their hoops.] Rest your hands in your laps and let your ears do the work for now."

Listening (Auditory and Kinesthetic)
Materials:

- Piano or other keyboard
- The "Jingle Bells" song for the teacher

Procedure:

1. "I am going to play our song, "Jingle Bells," on the piano. Listen to my solo. [Teacher plays the melody only.] Now I'm going to get fancy and add a lot of other sounds to our song. Listen to this. [Teacher plays the song with a thick, pronounced accompaniment.] Let's test your ears. When I play a solo [teacher plays a few notes of the melody], you'll hold up your thumb. When I play a lot of sounds or a group of them together [teacher models the thick accompaniment], you'll hold up both hands. Let's try it."

2. "Show me what you'll do when you hear my solo [teacher plays a few notes of the melody and checks the class for the thumb signal] and what you'll do when you hear many sounds or groups of sounds together [teacher plays the thick accompaniment and checks the class for raised hands]. You've got it! Now you are on your own. I won't help you. Do it on your own this time."

3. The teacher switches back and forth between the melody and the melody with thick accompaniment, monitoring the students' responses. "You did it without me! Yippee! You signaled the difference between the solo [teacher plays a few notes of the melody] and the groups of sounds [teacher plays accompaniment]. Nice work. You are ready to play solos on some instruments."

Performing (Auditory and Kinesthetic)
Materials:

- Unpitched percussion (tambourines, woodblocks, and sticks)

Procedure:

1. "Watch me as I walk over to the instruments. My choices today are the tambourine [teacher models this], the woodblock [models], or the sticks [models]. I'm going to choose the tambourine and carry it back to my seat without any noise. Notice that I'm putting it in my lap and holding it quietly until everyone gets an instrument."

2. "Skyler, please show the class how to choose one of those instruments—the tambourine, woodblock, or sticks—and carry it back to your seat. Watch Skyler rest it in her lap. . . . Thank you. Row 1, please do what Skyler did. I love it when you handle the instruments so carefully. Match Skyler and rest your instruments in your laps. . . . Row 2, please do the same thing . . . and row 3, show us how to do it. Thank you for resting your instruments. You do that as well as the fifth graders do."

3. "Let's practice. Get your instrument ready to play. I'll play a *solo* and you play it back to me as a *group*. [Teacher plays

61

a four-beat pattern and cues the class to echo, continuing for three different patterns.] You played exactly what I played."

4. "Let's try playing the words of our song, 'Jingle Bells.' I'll sing it and you play with me. Rea-dy and here we go. [Teacher sings and plays while the class plays along.] We just played as a group. John, please play the song as a solo. Rea-dy and here you go [he plays] and now everyone play it as group. Rea-dy and here you go. [The class plays it.] Everyone plays it as a group. Rea-dy and here you go. [The class plays it together.]"

5. After this is finished, the teacher segues to improvisation. "You get to do your own music this time. I'll point to one person to play a solo at a time. Everybody must rest your instrument while that solo is occurring. Be good, polite listeners."

Improvising, Composing, and Creating (Auditory and Kinesthetic)
Materials:

- Unpitched percussion (tambourines, woodblocks, and sticks)

Procedure:

1. The teacher starts by standing near one child and cues that child to play, cutting him or her off after four beats; the teacher proceeds around the room until each child has had a turn.

2. "Each of you played a solo today. Thank you for playing your solos and for handling your instruments carefully. Row 3, please show us how to walk to the shelf to return your instruments. Class, you'll notice they are not touching anybody or anything. . . . Row 2, please do that like row three did . . . and row 1, you know what to do. . . . You are wonderful listeners and did exactly what I asked. Thank you."

Reading and Writing (Visual and Auditory)
    Materials:

- Poster or slide of "Jingle Bells" with the pitches represented iconically

- Projector and screen

Procedure:

1. "Now that you know the difference between a solo and a group, let's look at the song, 'Jingle Bells,' that is on the screen." The teacher has a large poster or slide of the song with the pitches presented at different pitch levels—not on a staff—but with bell icons to designate the pitch levels and rhythm. "We have been working on reading music. The chart shows you the song. I will point to each bell and we can sing this together [teacher establishes the starting pitch and cue]. One, two rea-dy, sing." They sing together.

2. "You just sang it as a group with your voices singing together. Row 2, please sing it in your group [teacher gives the starting pitch and cue]. One, two, rea-dy, sing [row 2 sings it]. You sang together! Thank you. [Teacher sings this on the starting pitch.] Row 1, sing it in your group. Rea-dy and here you sing [they sing]. [Teacher sings this.] Thank you. Row 3, rea-dy and sing it now [they sing]. Very accurate singing in your rows, class."

3. "Now that we had different groups sing it, would you give me a 'thumbs up' if you would sing it as a solo? William, rea-dy and sing it now [teacher continues to point to the bell icons]. You sang your solo while I pointed to the bells, William. Another person ready to sing a solo? Kendra, rea-dy and sing it now [teacher points to the icons]. Another excellent solo, Kendra."

Closure and Check of Learning
"Today we learned about solos and groups."

- Identification: Teacher asks the class to hold up the number of fingers to show how many people sing a solo.

- Verbalization: Teacher asks a student to tell the class how many people could sing the song in a group (anything more than one is correct).

- Demonstration: Teacher asks the class to sing the song as a group, then one student to sing it as a solo.

- Further application: Teacher asks the students to think about things that are *solo* or in *groups* at home or outside and tell the class about it in the next music class (to maintain the focus on the concept and expect accountability).

LOTS
Singing the song as a group, moving their bodies, and recognizing differences between solos and groups in listening.

HOTS
Improvising on their instruments and reading the icons of the song.

The Lesson Model: Grade 1
Concept: *Long and short sounds as related to rhythm*, threaded through every segment of this lesson
National Standards:

1. Singing, alone and with others, a varied repertoire of music.

2. Performing on instruments, alone and with others, a varied repertoire of music.

3. Improvising melodies, variations, and accompaniments.

4. Reading and notating music.

5. Listening to, analyzing, and describing music.

Performing (Visual and Auditory)
Materials:

- Flashcard with the word *rhythm* on it

- Whiteboard, marker, and eraser

Procedure:

1. "Today we are going to learn to *read* music. I know you have been learning how to read words and sentences in your class, and now we're going to add music to your reading. We will have great fun looking at music, knowing that we will read short and long sounds."

2. "If you remember what we call the word in music that describes long and short sounds, please blink your eyes at me. Jon, please tell us the word that describes music's long and short sounds. You are correct. The word is *rhythm*. [The teacher shows a card with the vocabulary word on it.] Everyone please say that word with me. Rhy-thm."

3. "I am going to clap looong sounds. Please listen to my sounds and play them back to me [he or she plays four quarter notes]." The teacher plays four long sounds while simultaneously saying "next one" on the fourth beat. In other words, there is no dead time between the teacher's modeling and the class's echoes. "Now please play short sounds back to me." The teacher plays eight short sounds or eighth notes, giving verbal cues before he or she finishes so that the class responds without any unnecessary rests.

4. "You made very accurate long and short sounds. Let's try mixing them together. I will clap a pattern that has long *and* short sounds in it. [The teacher claps three more patterns using both long and short sounds in four-beat segments; the class echoes each one.] You are wonderful listeners and clapped exactly the correct rhythm each time."

5. "It's time to show you how to read these. I am going to use Laura's name and write the sound on the board [the teacher writes

two long dashes to represent 'Lau-ra,' then points to each dash as he or she says the name, repeating this two or three times]. Please read it with me and say her name [the teacher points and the class reads the icon]. Those were excellent long sounds."

6. "Ari's name has short sounds. Look at these [the teacher writes two dashes, pointing to each while saying 'A-ri' a few times]. Read these with me and we'll say his name three times. Rea-dy and here we read. A-ri, A-ri, A-ri. You are so accurate at reading the short sounds in his name."

7. "I am so curious to see if you can read long and short sounds mixed together. Look at this. I am writing Jon-a-thon [the teacher writes two dashes and one long dash and says his name one time while pointing to the icons]. Please read it with me. Rea-dy and go. Jon-a-thon. You did it! You are ready to read a song!"

Reading (Visual, Auditory, and Kinesthetic)
Materials:

- The song "Have You Seen My Honey Bears?" presented on a slide or poster that has iconic presentation of the rhythm

- Projector and screen

Procedure:

1. The teacher shows a slide of the short and long dashes, depicting the rhythm for the first verse of "Have You Seen My Honey Bears?" (traditional song, text by Rubin, 1988). "Use your eyes to notice where the short sounds are and where the long ones are. We will say 'short' on the short sounds and 'looong' on the long sounds. Let's try two lines together. Rea-dy and here we go. Short, short, short, short, short, short, looong, short, short, looong." The teacher points and speaks the first two lines with the class; if there are inaccuracies, he or she has the class practice clapping long sounds and short sounds before reading the lines again.

2. "I believe that you can read the next two lines without me. [The teacher gives a starting cue and points to each icon as the class reads the rhythm of the third and fourth lines.] Wow, you did it without me!"

3. "Here's another challenge: Read all four lines of the song without me and clap the long and short sounds. Rea-dy and here you go. [The teacher points to each dash and lets the class clap the rhythm.] You have already read the song we are going to sing. Very accurate reading, first grade."

Singing (Auditory and Visual)
Materials:

• Slide of "Have You Seen My Honey Bears?" with rhythmic icons and text

• Recording of "Have You Seen My Honey Bears?"

Procedure:

1. The teacher shows a slide of the first verse of "Have You Seen My Honey Bears?" that includes both the dash icons and the words. He or she asks the class to blurt the words as he or she points to them, ignoring the rhythm.

2. "Now that you know the words of the song, let's try reading the words with the long and short sounds. I will show you with the first two lines. [The teacher points to the icons and reads 'have you seen my hon-ey bears, hon-ey bears.'] Your turn to read it and speak the words. Rea-dy and go. [The teacher points to the icons as the class reads.] I think you're ready to read and speak the next two lines without me. Rea-dy and here you go. [The teacher points to the icons and the class speaks the words in rhythm.] You are so good at this that you are able to read two new lines of the song." The teacher prepares them by asking them to read the words of lines 5 and 6, then cues them to read them in rhythm.

3. "The last two lines of the song look a bit different, so please notice that there is a really long sound. [The rhythm of the last two lines contains a slur, so the rhythm must be designated by one very long dash to distinguish its length from the other notes.] I'll show you this because it's brand new. [The teacher points to the icons and speaks the rhythm of the remainder of the first verse.] Please read the last two lines with me. Ready and go." The class reads these as the teacher points to the icons.

4. "You read the entire song. I am impressed that you already know long and short sounds. Please get your bodies ready to listen to the song. Rest your lips, rest your hands, and open your ears. Use your eyes to read it while you hear the recording." The teacher plays a recording of the song while the class reads the icons on the slide.

5. "I will play it once more and this time I'll ask you to listen and read the song without my help. [The teacher plays the recording again while monitoring to see if the students are reading; if not, he or she must draw their focus to the song and help them to get on track.] I saw your eyes moving with the words. This time please read the song in your head while I sing it." The teacher models the song.

6. "Sing it with me. [The teacher establishes the starting pitch and sings the cue, 'rea-dy, sing,' on that pitch.] Please try it once more with me and then you'll do it on your own. [The teacher establishes the starting pitch and cues them to sing with him or her.] Excellent reading, first grade. This last time, let's sing it softer. You are reading without me. [The teacher reestablishes the starting pitch and has the class sing.] You read the long and short rhythm correctly and sang it more softly. Good music making, class."

Moving (Auditory and Kinesthetic)
Materials:

- Piano or other keyboard

Procedure:

1. "We are going to be moving around the room to long and short sounds. Your job will be to listen to long sounds that I play on the keyboard. When I play a looong sound, you will walk a looong note." The teacher models walking with a long step, then walking four of them.

2. "Later I will play short sounds and you will run in short steps to match the short sounds. [The teacher models running eight quick steps.] When the keyboard stops, you stop." The teacher models stopping in place.

3. "To do this we need only two rules: Everyone must keep their feet on the floor and avoid touching anybody or anything. If you understand the rules, please nod your head 'yes.' I expect that everyone will follow the rules or they will be asked to sit down."

4. "Without fussing or making noise, please stand up in front of your chairs. You may walk in any direction; just remember where your feet belong and what your hands need to do. Let's begin with long sounds. I'll play one and you take one long step. Here we go. [The teacher plays a long sound—a quarter note—and the class takes a step.] That was one sound."

5. "Now I'm ready to try two. Walk with my sounds. Here we go. [The teacher plays two long sounds and the class walks two long steps.] I think you're ready for many of them. Be sure to start with me and stop with me. Here we go." The teacher plays eight or ten long sounds and the class walks with them.

6. "You've mastered the long sounds. The short ones are tricky. You must be an excellent listener with these. I'll play two short sounds and you'll run two short steps and stop. Here we go. [The teacher plays two eighth notes and the class runs two steps.] Now I'll play four short sounds and you'll run four short steps and stop. Here we go." The teacher plays four eighth notes and the class runs four steps.

7. "Let's mix them up. Your ears will tell you to make long steps or short ones. Be careful to stop right with me." The teacher

plays different patterns of long and short sounds, then says "freeze" when he or she is ready to give the final directive.

8. "As you head back to your seats, listen carefully and make your feet follow my patterns. [The teacher deliberately focuses on long sounds to calm the class as they move toward their seats.] Great listening, class. You easily recognized the long sounds, the short sounds, and the times when there were no sounds."

Improvising, Composing, and Creating (Auditory and Kinesthetic)
Materials:

- Unpitched percussion instruments for the class

Procedure:

1. "You are going to be the teacher and I will be the first-grade student. In a moment you will get percussion instruments and your job will be to create a pattern that has long and short sounds. You'll play it for the class and we'll all be your echo. I bet you remember that percussion instruments are the ones that you gently hit or shake to make noise."

2. "Watch me walk over to the instruments, choose one, and carry it back to my seat without noise. I will rest with it until everyone has one. Another 'teacher' in the room needs to show us how to do this. Mr. Jackson, will you please demonstrate that to everyone? Watch as he shows us how to get the instrument, carry it carefully, and rest with it patiently. Thank you, Mr. Jackson."

3. "Third row of teachers, please get your instruments. You know what to do. Thank you for handling it so well. Row 2 of teachers, please do the same. I so appreciate everyone waiting patiently with your instruments. And row 1 of teachers, do this. You are very careful with the instruments. As teachers, you knew just what to do."

4. "Please pick up your instruments. You all have until the count of twenty to create your pattern and then I become your stu-

dent. Rea-dy and go. [The teacher times them and gives them a huge cut-off.] Please rest your instruments. As teachers, you would not be playing or making noise when someone else is presenting a pattern, so handle this."

5. "Miss Wong, please play your pattern and we'll all echo you." The teacher will need to cue the class to begin each echo pattern and proceeds until everyone has had a turn.

6. "I'll wave my magic wand to turn you back into first-grade students. Abracadabra. [He or she pantomimes this.] Wonderful patterns! You all created long and short sounds in your rhythm patterns."

Listening, Reading, and Writing (Auditory, Visual, and Kinesthetic)
Materials:

• Recorded examples of long and short rhythms

Procedure:

1. The teacher plays recorded examples of long sounds: a sustained chord on the keyboard, a sustained sound from a clock striking on the hour, and a whistle blowing. Then the teacher plays recorded examples of short sounds: several eighth notes on the woodblock, a quick scale on the keyboard, a ball bouncing, and a dog barking.

2. He or she prepares the class by saying, "Let's check your ears to see if they're working properly. I have some long sounds and some short sounds to play for you. With your invisible ink, please draw a long dash in the air when you hear a long sound and a short dash when you hear short sounds. Here is the first one." The teacher monitors this carefully to ensure the students are responding appropriately, then specifically verbalizes reinforcement such as "You drew a long sound" or "Yes, that one was a short one."

Closure and Check of Learning
"Today we worked with words that described something about the sounds in music."

- Verbalization: Teacher asks a student to share the word that means long and short sounds in music (*rhythm*).

- Identification: Teacher asks the class to use invisible ink to indicate a long sound (whistle blowing) and a short sound (dog barking) while he or she plays the sounds.

- Demonstration: Teacher asks the class to clap long sounds and then short sounds, providing starting cues for each.

- Further application: Teacher asks the students to listen to their favorite music at home and determine if the song has long and short sounds in it (to maintain the focus on the concept and expect accountability).

LOTS
Echoing the clapping patterns, moving to the patterns, and singing the song.

HOTS
Creating patterns and reading rhythmic icons.

The Lesson Model: Grade I
Concept: *So–mi as related to melody*, threaded through every segment of this lesson
National Standards:

1. Singing, alone and with others, a varied repertoire of music.

2. Performing on instruments, alone and with others, a varied repertoire of music.

3. Improvising melodies, variations, and accompaniments.

4. Reading and notating music.

5. Listening to, analyzing, and describing music.

Introduction (Visual, Auditory, and Kinesthetic)
Materials:

- The "Teddy Bear" song for the teacher

Procedure:

1. The teacher meets the students at the door and begins, "Step the beat to my song and follow your leaders to our places in the circle." The teacher sings the song "Teddy Bear" (traditional song adapted by Trinka, 1996) on a neutral syllable, such as "loo," until all students are in a circle in the center of the room.

2. The teacher sings "Do what I do" on *so* (*s*) and *mi* (*m*) and proceeds with vocal warm-up patterns that highlight the minor third interval (*s–m*). The teacher sings "Hel-lo, boys and girls" on only the notes *so* and *mi* (*s–m–s–s–m*, etc.) The students echo the greeting. The teacher sings "All sit down, please" on the *s–m–s–m* pattern. The students echo as they sit in place.

Moving (Auditory, Visual, and Kinesthetic)
Materials:

- The "Teddy Bear" song for the teacher

Procedure:

1. "I'll hum a mystery song that we learned last time, and you listen to see if you remember what it is. When you remember it, sing with me." The teacher hums "Teddy Bear," and the students aurally identify the song and sing.

2. "Sing just the first two 'teddy bears' and use your invisible marker in the air to point to how those notes are moving. Show me if they are the same or if they move down. [The students then sing the first four beats while they point higher for the *so* notes and lower for the *mi* notes in the space in front of them.] Excellent work showing that the sounds move down, class."

Singing (Auditory and Kinesthetic)
Materials:

- The "Teddy Bear" song for the teacher
- The "Rich Man, Poor Man" song for the teacher
- Ball

Procedure:

1. The teacher sings, "All stand up, please, and echo after me [he or she sings on the notes *so* and *mi*; the students echo the pattern as they stand]. Sing 'Teddy Bear' as I bounce my ball." He or she establishes the starting pitch and cue. The students sing as the teacher bounces a playground or other ball on the steady beat.

2. When the students finish, the teacher immediately begins to sing "Rich Man, Poor Man" (Choksy and Hein, 1978) using the same steady beat as "Teddy Bear." "Let's bounce pretend balls on the steady beat." The teacher and students use ball bouncing arm motions to demonstrate the steady beat.

3. "I'll give the ball to one student who can bounce it to me on the steady beat. Then I'll bounce it to the next person as we're singing. That person can bounce it back to me. We'll keep going until we get to the last word, 'thief.' The person who catches it on 'thief' is out. The next person gets the ball, and we'll start another turn. If you are 'out,' you will need to sit down where your feet are now and watch patiently while singing with us until the end of the game."

4. The teacher and students continue the elimination game for as many turns as time allows. The teacher asks these questions as he or she demonstrates same, descending, and ascending on "stay the same," "high to low," and "low to high": "Who can tell me *how* these notes are moving? Do they stay the *same* or do they move from *high* to low or *low* to high?" He or she indicates *same*, *high to low*, and *low to high* using his or her hand levels, then sings four beats on a neutral syllable (*s–m–s–m*).

5. "Navon, please sing the answer to me. [One student sings the high–low–high–low pattern.] Everyone, please touch your noses if you know what notes would be *so* and what ones would be *mi*?"

6. The teacher chooses one student to sing *so–mi–so–mi*, then he or she sings "You are right on" (*s–m–s–m*) followed by "First grade, sing now" as he or she leads them with the hand signs.

Reading and Writing (Visual and Kinesthetic)
Materials:

- The "Star Light, Star Bright" song for the teacher

- Piano, guitar, or recorder

- Whiteboard, marker, and eraser

- Magnetic stars

- Prepared note packets for each student

- The "Snail, Snail" song for the teacher

Procedure:

1. "Please use your listening ears. Everything is resting except your ears." The teacher plays "Star Light, Star Bright" (English nursery song adapted by Choksy, 1988) on a melodic instrument, such as piano, guitar, or recorder. "If you know the song, touch your elbow. Sam, please tell us the name of the song."

2. "Everyone, with your invisible marker, point to how these notes are moving." Teacher sings the first four beats on "star light, star bright" while the students point to the melodic contour (high–low–high–low) as above. The teacher draws a horizontal line on the board.

3. "Who can take these stars and make them match what we just sang? Let's put the high notes above the line and the low notes below the line. Wiggle your nose if you can do this for the class.

[The teacher gives four magnetic star icons to one student, who arranges them high–low–high–low.] Musicians call the high notes *so* and the low notes *mi*. Let's sing it with those names."

4. The teacher establishes the starting pitch and cue and the students sing the pattern *so–mi–so–mi*. "Musicians use special hand signs when they sing these two notes. [The teacher shows the hand signs for *so* and *mi*.] Let's sing it with the names and the special hand signs."

5. The students sing the pattern and demonstrate the hand signs while the teacher monitors their accuracy. "You sang the high and low sounds on the correct pitches and gave the correct hand signs for those sounds. Nice work, class."

6. The teacher has prepared note packets for each student. Each note packet should have four quarter notes, note heads, or icons along with one long, vertical line that represents a staff line for reference to higher and lower.

7. He or she sings directions to the class as they walk to the designated spot to get their packets. "I'll sing a song while you get your note packets. Be in your place with your packets after four times through." The teacher sings "Snail, Snail" (Choksy, 1981) four times as the students retrieve note packets and return to their places. This song has a tone set of *mi*, *so*, and *la* only, for isolating the pattern *s–m–s–m* on the words "Snail, snail, snail, snail" at the beginning.

8. "Sing the song while you get out your notes and your line. Let's figure out how these notes are moving. This time, keep your answer inside your head. [The teacher sings first four beats ('Snail, snail, snail, snail').] Let's point with our eyes how those notes are moving. Look up for *so* notes and down for *mi* notes." The students derive the pattern of *s–m–s–m*, looking up and down appropriately.

9. "Use your notes to write the pattern you just showed me with your eyes. [The students lay notes down higher and lower than the vertical line.] Let's sing it and check our work. Please point to the notes as we sing." The teacher establishes the starting

pitch and cue, then the students sing the first four beats and point to the notes.

10. "How many times through the song do you think it will take us to put away our notes and lines, put the packets away, and return to our seats? [One student gives an answer. The teacher leads them to try for a lower number. The students put their materials away as they sing the song.] Did we make it?" The students answer "yes" or "no." The teacher responds with either "Hurray!" or "Maybe next time."

Performing (Visual, Auditory, and Kinesthetic)
Materials:

- The "Star Light, Star Bright" song for the teacher
- The "Snail, Snail" song for the teacher
- The "Rich Man, Poor Man" song for the teacher
- The "Dinah" song for the teacher

Procedure:

1. "Last time in music we sang 'Star Light, Star Bright.' I'm curious to see if you can figure out the pattern from 'Star Light, Star Bright.' [Students answer, '*s–m–s–m*'; the teacher then repeats question with 'Rich Man, Poor Man' and 'Snail, Snail.'] Does anyone notice anything about those three patterns?" The students answer, "They're the same." "You are so correct."

2. "I'll sing a new song. Listen for today's *so* and *mi* pattern." The teacher sings "Dinah" (Choksy, 1981). In this song, there is a prominent *s–m–s–m* pattern on the words, "Dinah, Dinah," that repeat throughout the song.

3. "Where were our new notes? [The students answer, 'Dinah, Dinah.'] Let's sing our own names instead Dinah's name." To practice, the teacher sings the song, and the students sing their own names on the "Dinah" pattern of *s–m–s–m*.

4. "Who would like to sing it for the class? [Teacher allows individuals to sing their names as time allows.] Thank you for

using your good singing voices to match the *so* and *mi* sounds today."

Improvising, Composing, and Creating (Visual, Auditory, and Kinesthetic)
Materials:

- Barred instruments with either tonic and dominant or so and mi set up

Procedure:

1. "In just a minute, I want you to find a partner. Quickly and quietly, without fussing, you and your partner will move to a barred instrument in the room and sit down with your hands in your lap. You've got until the count of ten to do all of that. I won't hear any noise as you do this, so handle it quietly and quickly." The teacher counts to ten while the students follow those directions.

2. "Decide who will be partner 1 and partner 2. Partners 1, you will pick up your mallets. Remember that we hold the mallets with 'pinch and curl.' Pick up the mallets correctly and show me playing position." Ideally, a tonic bass bar would provide the bass. If one is not available, bass xylophones can be set up with the tonic in octaves or the tonic and dominant notes. All other instruments are set up with only *so* and *mi* bars.

3. "I want the bass instruments to play the steady beat on their bars. The rest of us will play whatever we want [improvise] four beats using *so* and *mi*. Let's play them and figure out which one is *so* and which one is *mi*." The students experiment and decide the smaller bar is *so* and the larger bar is *mi*.

4. "Let's start with four beats of the bass line, and then partners 1 can improvise four beats with our two notes." The students improvise all at the same time for practice several times before improvising in smaller groups and then individually as time permits. The teacher repeats the process with the other partners.

Listening (Visual and Auditory)
Materials:

- Either the "Lady, Lady" song or a recording of it

Procedure:

1. "Quickly and quietly, put your mallets away and move to your listening spot. [The students follow instructions appropriately and sit in their listening spots in the room.] Please sit with your hands in your lap and your eyes on me. This is what a good audience does when they listen to music."

2. "You're going to be an audience as I sing a song with *so* and *mi*. See if you can find the two new notes, and raise your hand on the words that have *so* and *mi*." The teacher either performs or plays a recording of "Lady, Lady" (Trinka, 1989a, 1989b). This song has a prominent *s–m–s–m* pattern on the words "lady, lady" that begin the song and are repeated later.

3. "Who can tell me the words that had *so* and *mi*? [A student answers, 'lady, lady.'] Let's sing those words using our new hand signs for *so* and *mi*. [The teacher establishes the starting pitch and cue and leads the class in singing the song.] Excellent job singing the *so* and *mi* pitches accurately."

Closure and Check of Learning (Visual, Auditory, and Kinesthetic)
"Today we sang songs that had a new pattern in them."

- Identification: Teacher asks students to give a "thumbs up" when he or she sings the higher note (*so*) and a "thumbs down" when he or she sings the lower note (*mi*).

- Verbalization: Teacher asks the class to blurt the name the two new notes (*so* and *mi*).

- Demonstration: Teacher asks the class to sing the *s–m–s–m* pattern and show the correct hand signs with the sounds.

- Further application: The teacher asks the class to listen to their favorite song at home and see if it has the *so* and *mi* pattern in it.

LOTS
Identifying, singing, and performing the hand signs *so* and *mi.*

HOTS
Writing the pattern with notes and/or icons and improvising the accompaniment.

The Lesson Model: Grade 2
Concept: *Rhythm*, threaded through every segment of this lesson
National Standards:

1. Singing, alone and with others, a varied repertoire of music.

2. Performing on instruments, alone and with others, a varied repertoire of music.

3. Improvising melodies, variations, and accompaniments.

4. Reading and notating music.

5. Listening to, analyzing, and describing music.

6. Understanding music in relation to history and culture.

Introduction (Visual, Auditory, and Kinesthetic)
Materials: None

Procedure:

1. The teacher begins, "We are going to focus on the word *rhythm* today and have you create your own rhythms. First, let's review what that word means. If you remember what it means, give me a 'thumbs up.' I'll ask Bella to tell us what it means. Yes, it means sounds can be short or long."

2. "Jim, clap a loooong sound for us. Thank you. Everyone do that with me. Rea-dy and clap [teacher and class clap together]. Everyone clap four long sounds with me. Rea-dy and clap [all do it together]. Arielle, clap short sounds for us. Thank you. Everyone clap eight short sounds with me. Rea-dy and clap." They all do it together.

3. "We have just clapped long and short sounds that make rhythm, but we're going to use our names to make these more interesting today. I'll clap my name: Mis-ter Jones [repeating it three times to establish the pattern]. Try that with me. Ready and clap [all do it together]. Let's try your names."

4. The teacher walks to each student, makes eye contact, and claps the first name with the class echoing. He or she will need to give firm cues for entrances and exits to exhibit precision, such as "rea-dy, clap."

Reading and Writing (Visual and Kinesthetic)
Materials:

- Iconic chart of rhythm showing the teacher's name
- Whiteboard, marker, and eraser

Procedures:

1. The teacher shows the class an iconic representation of short (two eighths) and long (quarter) notes with dashes (- - —) to demonstrate his or her name (Mr. Jones). "Class, look at the short–short–long pattern that I've written to show you the rhythm of my name. I'll point to it and say my name. Please watch. Mis-ter Jones."

2. "Let's try some of your names. Blair, how do you think we'd write your name? Does it have short–short sounds or does it have long sounds? [The teacher will need to say her name a few times for her to determine it is a long sound.] You are correct. It is a long sound. I'll write it. Class, please say her name as I point to the long rhythm [a long dash on the board]."

3. Teacher asks the class to identify the pattern for a few of the students' names and writes those on the board or has students do so. Teacher points as the class reads and claps these patterns, establishing starting cues.

4. "Watch what happens as I change our dashes to music notes. For every long sound I'm going to erase it and replace it with

a quarter note. Please read these with me again. Rea-dy, go. [The teacher points to the rhythm as the class reads and claps them.] You were so accurate in clapping the quarter notes."

5. "Now you're ready for the eighth notes. We will see them hooked together in pairs. I will replace all of the short–short dashes with a pair of eighth notes. [The teacher adds the eighth notes, then repeats the cues to have the class read all the rhythms with only eighth and quarter notes.] You are so good at reading music already! Very accurate rhythm reading, class. And you already have read some of the rhythm in our song for today."

Moving (Auditory and Kinesthetic); Improvising, Composing, and Creating (Visual, Auditory, and Kinesthetic)
Materials: None

Procedure:

1. "Now that you have heard the rhythm of your names, we're going to use your whole body to create a rhythm of your name. For instance, if I were to use my name, Mis-ter Jones, I would need to make two short movements for 'Mis-ter' and one long one for 'Jones.' It might look like this." Teacher waves his or her hands back and forth like windshield wipers for the short movements and moves his or her head from a tall position to looking at his or her stomach for a long one.

2. "Let's use one of you for demonstration. Kyle, please come here and we'll have Jennifer tell us whether we need short movements or long ones for Kyle's name. Yes, that is correct, we need a long one. Joe, what could Kyle do to show his long movement with his body? Yes, he could jump high. Kyle, let's try that as I say your name. [Kyle jumps as the teacher says, 'Kyyyllllle.'] Breanna, what other choice could Kyle make with a long movement? Yes, he could swish his body like a hula. Kyle, please try that one while I say your name. [The teacher repeats the process.] Those are great choices. Kyle, you may sit down."

3. "Since Kyle's name had one looong sound, let's practice one that uses short sounds and see what it looks like. Tiffany, please

come here. Let me say your name twice while the class listens to the pattern of sounds. Tif-fan-y, Tif-fan-y. David, would you please say her name twice? [The teacher has the child say it to allow for more opportunities to hear the pattern.] Thank you. Madison, what movements could she do to show two short sounds for 'Tif' and 'fan'? Oh, I like that. She could wiggle down and up. And now we need a long sound for the end of her name, 'yyyyy.' Charles, what could she do with her body to show a looong sound? Yes, she can stretch up high with her hands."

4. "Class, when I say 'go,' you will quickly and quietly stand up in your space without touching anything. I will give you twenty seconds to practice *your name* with your whole body movements and then we'll see some of your ideas. Rea-dy and go!"

5. It is important for the teacher to monitor what the class is doing, check for accuracy, and watch the clock. If too much time elapses, the students will start to create discipline problems because they will have lost their focus. Keep them on task by giving them only the time needed for this. For instance, by giving them only twenty seconds, they know they do not have time to waste; in contrast, giving them two minutes would allow many problems to occur. The teacher will need to see if everyone is done in twenty seconds, and if not, give them ten to fifteen more seconds. But as soon as they are finished, he or she needs to redirect them.

6. The teacher will ask several students to demonstrate their names through body movements and focuses the class on watching the performer and using good manners. The teacher needs to remind them to be quiet listeners, to be respectful of the performer, and to be polite.

7. The teacher needs to finish with a student who has the same rhythm as his or her name so that the segue to the next experience becomes the transition between activities. Let's assume the teacher uses his or her own name. "Class, watch me do my movement and tell me what the sounds look like, short or long. [The teacher performs his or her movement version of short–short–long.] Please blurt the pattern. [The class says,

'short–short–long.'] You are right on. We're going to use that pattern in our song today, so be ready to find that pattern."

Singing (Auditory and Kinesthetic)
Materials:

- Textbooks for the class and the teacher that contain the song "Yankee Doodle"

Procedure:

1. "Carefully, quickly, and quietly take out your books and find page [fill in the blank]. Let's practice doing that without any noise [teacher models it for them and rehearses it with them if it does not occur without noise]. Thank you for doing that as I asked."

2. "John, please read the title of the song. Thank you. 'Yankee Doodle' [traditional song] is an American song that was used when the soldiers marched with George Washington. It's well over two hundred years old."

3. "If you will look at the beginning of the song, you might notice that the rhythm looks familiar [it is the eighth-note pairs and quarter note rhythm pattern they just read]. Please take your finger and tap the rhythm as I sing the verse to you." The rhythm changes for the refrain, so stop ahead of that.

4. The teacher sings it with attention to the rhythm, then asks the class to clap the rhythm of the verse as he or she sings it again. He or she hums it as the class claps the rhythm, then instructs them to rest their hands while he or she sings the verse to them again and they echo it.

5. After the class has command of singing the verse, they are asked to think the words in their heads and clap their rhythm aloud. The teacher teaches the refrain of the song and has the class clap its rhythm. Finally, the class sings and claps the rhythm of the entire song. "You have learned to read, clap, and sing the rhythm of the song today. Very accurate reading, class."

Performing (Visual, Auditory, and Kinesthetic)
  Materials:

- Barred instruments (xylophones and metallophones) and appropriate mallets, one per person

- Poster with iconic and symbolic rhythmic patterns on it

- The "Lucy Locket" song for the teacher

Procedure:

1. The teacher has the C pentaton already set on the barred instruments on the floor of the classroom. The students are seated elsewhere in the room either on the floor or in chairs. The teacher models what will happen before the students move to the instruments so that they see and hear all directions before touching the instruments.

2. "Today we are going to use the xylophones [briefly plays a few keys] and the metallophones [plays a bit]. You will need to use one mallet and handle these professionally with your elbows out to the side like this. You'll remember that we handle the mallets with 'pinch and curl.' The reason we hold the mallets this way is so that they can strike the key and then bounce off [demonstrates]. If the mallet doesn't bounce, the sound is dead like this." He or she demonstrates the "thud" sound.

3. "With your *air* xylophone, please pick up your *air* mallets and try this with me [rehearsing how to hold the mallets and strike the keys in the air]. When we play today, you'll be able to use any of the keys, but you need to play the rhythm we have been using for my name."

4. "Here is the pattern [shows a poster of the icons and symbols for the ostinato, a pair of eighths and a quarter with a repeat sign]. You will play this pattern over and over on any keys. Let me show you." He or she demonstrates.

5. "As we get ready to move to the instruments, you will please *walk around* them [teacher models this as he or she talks about it], sit down behind one, and rest your mallets [teacher models

this]. We'll play together. When I say 'go,' handle this without any noise." Teacher gently says "go" and has the class move to the instruments. If they do not handle this as per instructions, have them return to the seats, then remodel what you want from them before having them move again. They can do this, but the teacher has to be persistent in expecting it and in monitoring what they do to achieve this.

6. The teacher will model picking up the mallet and putting it into playing position, and have the students echo this. Teacher instructs the class to play the short–short–long pattern on one key and cues them to begin in tempo. They rehearse it a few times and then he or she cues them to stop.

7. "Now we're ready to play that rhythm with an old favorite song, 'Lucy Locket' [traditional song]. Use any keys you want, just keep the pattern going until we all stop together. Let's practice that. One, two, rea-dy, go." The class plays the ostinato together, and when they have successfully played the pattern in sync, the teacher sings the song.

8. He or she may have the boys sing and girls play, then reverse it to check their accuracy. "We were all together at exactly the same tempo. Very good playing and listening, class. Please carefully lay your mallets down and walk back to your places without any noise."

Listening (Visual, Auditory, and Kinesthetic)
Materials:

- Picture of Pyotr Tchaikovsky

- Recording of *The Nutcracker Suite*

- World map or globe

Procedure:

1. "You have just played rhythm and now we're going to listen to a wonderful part from *The Nutcracker Suite* [Tchaikovsky, written in 1891–1892]. Here is a picture of the composer,

Mr. Pyotr Tchaikovsky, who lived in Russia between 1840 and 1893. I'll show you where Russia is on the map [teacher points to it and then traces his or her finger to the town where the students' school is] and where we live. Please get your ears ready for listening, rest your lips, and hear just a bit of this and please notice the rhythm—long and short sounds."

2. Teacher plays part of the "Overture"—around twenty-five seconds—so that the class hears the predominant rhythmic pattern that occurs. He or she then claps the designated pattern to the class a few times, humming the melodic element, then has the class show a "thumbs up" when they hear the pattern in the music. He or she plays around thirty-five seconds of the piece. "Jill, what do we call that part of the piece that I clapped and you identified? *Rhythm* is correct."

Closure and Check of Learning (Visual, Auditory, and Kinesthetic)
"Today we learned about long and short sounds."

- Identification: Teacher asks a member of the class to find an example of rhythm in the room.

- Verbalization: Teacher asks the class to blurt (concerted attention to getting a group response) the word that describes long and short sounds (*rhythm*).

- Demonstration: Teacher asks two students to clap the rhythm of their names for the class.

- Further application: Teacher asks them to find something that has rhythm at home and tell the class about it in the next music class (to maintain the focus on the concept and expect accountability).

LOTS
Echoing the teacher with clapping and singing.

HOTS
Creating the rhythm of their names through movement and reading the rhythm iconically and symbolically.

The Lesson Model: Grade 2

Concept: *Harmony*, threaded through every segment of this lesson

National Standards:

1. Singing, alone and with others, a varied repertoire of music.

2. Performing on instruments, alone and with others, a varied repertoire of music.

3. Composing and arranging music within specified guidelines.

4. Reading and notating music.

5. Listening to, analyzing, and describing music.

Introduction (Visual and Auditory)

Materials:

- Pictures of "harmonious" and "unharmonious" scenes

- Flashcard with the word *harmony* on it

Procedure:

1. The teacher begins by saying, "We have an interesting task today. I'm going to show you some pictures and ask if the things in the picture belong together." He or she shows them pictures of *obvious* ideas that mesh, such as a street of houses with children playing in the yards and those that do not mesh, such as a clown performing for animals in a barnyard or a landscape of mountains and a river running through (but running through a person's house). Another option could be using clothing items such as an evening dress with tennis shoes, pajamas with boots, and a well-coordinated outfit.

2. "I will show the pictures again and ask you to give me a 'thumbs up' if you think the things belong together and a 'thumbs down' if they do not." The teacher proceeds with showing the pictures in the same order and checking the responses.

3. "If the things in the picture do not belong together we might describe those are being silly or not making sense; if the things belong together we might say they work in *harmony*. That is our new word for today. When something has harmony, the things work well together."

4. "We are going to experience harmony with our bodies and our voices today. [The teacher shows the vocabulary word on a sign with *harmony* printed on it.] Please say the word with me. Har-mo-ny. That's the word for the day."

Moving (Kinesthetic and Visual)
Materials: None

Procedure:

1. "Notice that I am walking over to the open floor and that I'm not touching anything. When I get to my place, I begin to form a circle and wait patiently. Josie, please do the same thing and show the class how to handle this. [Josie walks over to add to the circle.] Row 3, please do exactly what Josie did and find your personal space in the form of a circle with us. . . . Row 2, please do that . . . and row 1, finish it, please. Thank you for handling it so well."

2. "Please watch as I show you how we're going to use harmony to-day. For the moment, Kara will be my partner. She will watch as I take four beats to move my body, then I will stand still and she'll use her body to 'echo' mine. So, I move four beats [teacher models doing the twist, one movement that is easily echoed], then Kara takes four beats to echo me." Kara imitates the movement.

3. "Without noise, find a partner next to you with whom you can work. Please do that by the time I count to three. One, two, three. [The teacher finds anyone without a partner and matches him or her with remaining students or with him- or herself.] The partner who is the shortest goes first, taking four beats to do *one* move. And it must be one move so that the other partner can echo you. Partners 1, let's practice. Rea-dy,

and here you go. One, two, three, four." Partners designated as "number 1" move.

4. "Now it's partner number 2's turn. Partners 2, rea-dy and here you echo. One, two, three, four [partners 2 echo]. You remembered the moves very well. Let's switch. Partners 2 now lead and partners 1 echo." The teacher repeats the process.

5. "You are so good at following your partners! Let's add another challenge to this. Partners 2 lead this. He or she will be moving for four beats *while* the other partner follows for those four beats. Let's try this *together*. Make one move and let your partner echo you. Rea-dy and here we go. One, two, three, four." The partners move together.

6. "Let's switch it now. Partners 1 lead and the other partners follow. Ready and here we go. One, two, three, four [the partners move together]. What you just did was to move in harmony. What you did fit together. But let's add yet another challenge to this."

7. "Partners 1, move for four beats in one direction while partners 2 move in a different direction. Each of you must stay in your own personal space, but you'll be doing different things at the same time. Rea-dy and here we go. One, two, three, four." The partners move at the same time.

8. "That was another example of harmony. While you moved differently, your movements fit together at the same time. If you move back to your seats without noise, we will sing harmony." The class moves to their seats without noise and the teacher acknowledges that they did what was asked.

Singing (Auditory)
Materials:

- The "Row, Row, Row Your Boat" song for the teacher

Procedure:

1. "To make harmony with our bodies, we needed more than one person. It takes at least two people doing things at the same

time to make harmony. So, to make harmony in music, we need to have more than one person, too."

2. "You probably remember the song 'Row, Row, Row Your Boat' [traditional song] that we have sung other days. Let's review it together." The teacher establishes the starting pitch, and, in tempo, sings the starting cue, "rea-dy, sing." The class sings the song once and the teacher determines if they need any more rehearsal. If not, he or she proceeds. "When we all sing the same thing together, we are singing the melody or the tune of the song."

3. "But now we're going to create harmony. That means that you are going to sing the song without me. I will be your echo and sing four beats later than you. So you'll sing once through the song and stop. This is the first time you'll hear me tell you not to sing with me. I'm going to sing *after* you, behind you, later than you, not with you. Because you're singing different sounds than I am at the same time, we'll make harmony. Let's try it." The teacher establishes the starting pitch and cues the class to sing, starting him- or herself four beats later.

4. "You did it! Let's do it once more, only let's take a little faster tempo. [He or she establishes the pitch and repeats the process.] We made harmony! You're ready for the next challenge."

5. "This half of the room [the teacher indicates with his or her hand] will sing first, leading, and the other half follows with me, being the echo." The teacher establishes the pitch and cues the groups to begin. If they handle it easily, he or she switches the groups; if they have difficulty, the teacher slows it down a bit and re-rehearses it. When they demonstrate ease with this, the teacher forms three groups by having each row sing a three-part round.

6. "What you just did was to sing in three parts, so we call that 'three-part harmony' since there are three groups singing at different times. You did an excellent job singing with your group and singing something different from the other groups."

CHAPTER FOUR

Performing (Auditory and Kinesthetic)
Materials:

- Unpitched percussion for the class

Procedure:

1. "You just sang three-part harmony, but now we're going to play it on instruments [unpitched percussion]. You remember how to handle getting the instruments. We do this without making a fuss or noise and then we play when everyone has one. Watch while I do this [the teacher gets an instrument, takes it back to his or her seat, and rests it]. Row 2, please get a percussion instrument, carry it back to your seats, and rest it in your laps. . . . Row 1, please do the same thing. Oh, I like the way everyone is handling the instruments carefully and gently. Row 3, please do that, too. . . . Thank you for following those directions so that our instruments do not get broken."

2. "Everyone, get your instrument ready to play and then freeze. Think the words in your head and we'll play the rhythm of the words together. Rea-dy and here we go." The class plays the song's rhythm together.

3. "Now we'll divide into groups to make harmony with it. Row 1, you'll play the rhythm of the words to 'Row, Row, Row' as group 1; row 2, you'll follow four beats behind them as group 2; and row 3, you'll follow four beats behind and play as group 3." The teacher cues each group and then gives a cut-off for each one.

4. "You just played three-part harmony, but let's do it in six parts this time. [The teacher designates six groups, cues them to begin, and gives cut-offs for each one.] That was six-part harmony. Wow, that was neat! You played exactly at the right time and with your group."

5. "Please lay your instruments down under your seat. These will rest for several minutes while we write rhythms and create our own harmony. You will play these later, but not now."

Reading and Writing; Improvising, Composing, and Creating (Auditory, Visual, and Kinesthetic)
Materials:

- Markers and paper for the class

- Whiteboard, marker, and eraser

Procedure:

1. "Since we have six groups, we will have each group write four beats of rhythm. In your group, you will move to a place on the floor and I will give you a marker and a sheet with measure lines. Your job is to decide as a group what rhythm you want to write for four beats. You can use quarter notes [the teacher writes one on the board and claps it as a reminder], quarter rests [writes one and demonstrates silence by pulling his or her hands apart to 'show' the rest], or a pair of eighth notes [writes a beamed pair and claps them]."

2. "While I point to the quarter note, blurt out how many counts it gets [one]. While I point at the quarter rest, show me with your fingers how many beats we rest on a quarter rest [one]. And with the eighth notes, blurt out how many counts the two notes get together [one]. You are ready."

3. "Carefully and quietly move with your group to a place on the floor by the time I count to three [the teacher counts with his or her fingers rather than out loud so that the class is reminded of a noise-free move]. Please look at me and smile if you can hear my voice." The teacher speaks in a very gentle voice to remind them to listen.

4. "As a group, you have two minutes to decide how to write your four beats of rhythm. One person in your group will be the scribe and write the rhythm in the measure on the paper. When I clap two times, it will be your signal to freeze. Nod your heads if you understand the directions [the class nods]."

5. The teacher monitors each group and times them, stopping as close to two minutes as possible, or before that if they are

finished. He or she claps twice and scans the group to ensure they are "frozen." "I see that everyone has four beats of rhythm written in your measures."

6. "Our next step is to appoint a conductor for each group, someone different from the scribe. The conductor will do my job in saying 'one, two, rea-dy, play' and all of you will clap your written rhythm together. You have until the count of four to appoint a conductor in your group." The teacher again counts on his or her fingers and gives them a cut-off. "Conductors, please count four beats and rehearse the rhythm with your group." The groups rehearse and the teacher immediately repeats this for a second rehearsal.

7. "I will collect your measures of rhythm, post them on the board, and we'll all rehearse all four measures. Please wait patiently while I do this. While you are waiting, practice the rhythms with a one-finger clap." The teacher posts them, then cues them to clap all four measures, giving a cut-off at the end.

8. "We will need to show that our piece has an end, so I'm going to draw a double bar at the end. That's the signal that we're finished playing. Let's try playing the entire piece together." The teacher cues them and they clap the measures together.

9. "Now we'll try our piece in two-part harmony. Please get your instruments carefully and quietly. For a moment, we'll go back to only two groups as we did when we started today. Group 1 [the teacher reminds the class by waving to each group] begins while group 2 starts four beats later. Everybody reads our new piece, but reads it with your group. Group 1, rea-dy, and here you go." He or she cues them to begin, then cues group 2, giving a cut-off at the end.

10. "You played it well, read your rhythm accurately, and stopped with your group. Let's jump to six-part harmony, so you'll play with your group, but with six groups starting and ending at different times." The teacher has the class rejoin their groups, then cues and gives cut-offs.

11. "Excellent reading of the rhythm, class. You handled starting and stopping with your own group. I'm impressed that you

could move, sing, play, and write harmony. We are going to put away our instruments quietly and carefully. Please rest them in your laps. Row 1, please show everyone else how to do this. . . . Row 3, please do the same . . . and row 2, you know what to do. Thank you for your good work in putting the instruments away quietly."

Closure and Check of Learning

"Today we learned a new word that describes sounds working well together at the same time."

- Verbalization: Teacher asks a student to share the new word with the class (*harmony*).

- Identification: Teacher asks the class to hold up the number of fingers to show how many sounds are needed to occur at the same time before harmony can occur (two or more).

- Demonstration: Teacher asks the class to clap their piece in two-part harmony without any assistance other than cueing the start of each group.

- Further application: Teacher asks the students to listen to their favorite music at home and determine if the song has harmony (to maintain the focus on the concept and expect accountability).

LOTS

Singing the song as a group, identifying the number of counts for various notes and rests, and recognizing the number of sounds needed in harmony.

HOTS

Reading, writing, and creating harmony.

The Lesson Model: Grade 2

Concept: *Melody*, threaded through every segment of this lesson

1. Singing, alone and with others, a varied repertoire of music.

2. Performing on instruments, alone and with others, a varied repertoire of music.

3. Composing and arranging music within specified guidelines.

4. Reading and notating music.

5. Listening to, analyzing, and describing music.

Introduction (Visual, Auditory, and Kinesthetic)
Materials:

- Piano or other keyboard

Procedure:

1. The teacher begins: "Today we are going to focus on the melody of a song. If you know what a melody is, give me a 'thumbs up.' Great! Who can *tell* me what a melody is? Right, it is a pattern of high and low sounds."

2. "I'm going to play a note on the piano. Give me a 'thumbs up' if it's a high note or a 'thumbs down' if it's a low note. [The teacher plays four or five different notes until he or she is satisfied that the students are accurately identifying the high and low notes.] You accurately indicated high notes [the teacher plays one or two] and low notes [plays one or two]. Good listening, class."

Listening (Visual, Auditory, and Kinesthetic) and Moving (Kinesthetic and Auditory)
Materials:

- Recording of the song "I Have a Car"

- The "I Have a Car" song for the teacher

Procedure:

1. The teacher prepares the class to identify particular sounds in a song by saying, "You have just identified high and low sounds. You're now going to listen to a fun song called 'I Have a Car' [No author, McGraw Hill, 2005] and you have two jobs to do while listening quietly. In your head you will figure out what

the car sounds are and remember them because I'll later ask you to identify if they're high or low sounds. Let's prepare to listen. Your lips are resting, your body is resting, and your ears are open wide. Thank you for getting ready."

2. "Listen for the sounds and remember if they're high or low. [The teacher plays a recording of the song and then has the class name the car sounds, calling on one person at a time to respond.] Alaina, please name one sound you heard in the song. Hong, please tell us if it's a high sound or a low sound. You are both correct. Jeremy, what is another sound you heard? Ricardo, is that one high or low? You identified those expertly." The teacher continues until the honk, rattle, crash, and beep are identified.

3. "We are going to add some body motions pretending to drive the car. Let me show you. When we hear the honk, we will pull an imaginary lever similar to the ones in a semi-truck like this. [Teacher demonstrates and cues the class to echo it.] When we hear the rattle, we will shake the lower half of our body like a rattle. [Teacher demonstrates.] Do it with me. When the car crashes, we will clap like this. [Teacher demonstrates.] Try it with me. And when we hear the beep, we will touch our noses. Try that one with me."

4. "Let's try a honk [teacher leads the class], a rattle, a crash, and a beep. Let's do it once more to make it perfect. You are ready to perform those with the music. Please get ready to listen again and our bodies will do the honks, rattles, crashes, and beeps with the song."

5. The teacher plays the song again, leading them in performing. "You put the body moves in just the right places, class. Very good listening. We're going to sing the melody and work on the high and low sounds in it."

Singing (Auditory and Kinesthetic) and Moving (Kinesthetic and Auditory)
Materials:

- The "I Have a Car" song for the teacher

- Flashcard with the word *phrase* on it

Procedure:

1. The teacher teaches the students the melody of the verse by echo singing. "I will sing a small part called a *phrase* to you and you'll repeat it back to me. [The teacher shows the vocabulary word on a card to the class.] Say it with me, please. Phrase. Yes, that's it."

2. "Let me sing a phrase and then you can sing it back to me. [He or she models a phrase, establishes the starting pitch, and cues students to repeat it.] Now that you have sung the phrases, let's sing all of the phrases together for the whole song. [The teacher establishes the starting pitch and cues them to sing.] You sang all of the phrases! I liked the high and low pitches in your melody."

3. "Let's explore more about the high and low sounds. We have used scales before to show how the melody moves higher and lower, but today we're going to use our bodies to show those pitches. For instance, our toes will be *do*. [The teacher sings *do* and touches his or her toes.] When we sing *re* we will touch our knees." The teacher sings *re* and touches his or her knees, followed by *mi* touching the hips, *so* touching the shoulders, and *la* touching the head.

4. "I'll sing a phrase using *do*, *re*, *mi*, *so*, and *la* while showing the pitches on my body; please be my mirror and perform these back to me. Without fussing or making noise, stand up and get your bodies ready. Thank you." The teacher demonstrates each phrase, then establishes the starting pitch and cue for the class to echo.

5. "I'm wondering if you can tell which one is the highest sound in the song. If you know it, tap your knee. Juan, please tell us what the highest sound is. Yes, it is *la*. Hmm. I'm wondering what the lowest sound is. Blink your eyes if you know this. Jenny, what is the lowest sound? *Do* is correct."

6. "Let's put the real words back into the song. I'll sing a phrase to you and you echo it. Here is the starting pitch." The teacher gives the pitch and cue.

7. "I think you are ready to put the movements into the song for the honk, rattle, crash, and beep. Let's sing and do the movements. [The teacher establishes the starting pitch and cue.] You did the entire song with high and low pitches! I'm so happy you're able to control your voices to make the different sounds of the melody."

Performing (Visual, Auditory, and Kinesthetic); Improvising, Composing, and Creating (Visual, Auditory, and Kinesthetic)
Materials:

- Unpitched percussion instruments for the class

Procedure:

1. The teacher has the students choose an instrument for each car sound and improvise the way it will produce that car sound. To prepare the students for the task, he or she says, "We are about to choose instruments for the honks, rattles, crashes, and beeps. We will need to select instruments that make the appropriate high and low sounds."

2. "To do this, you are going to become detectives. I will establish a team of four people. Each team will have one minute to go to the instruments, find an appropriate one for your sound, and then sit down in your group with your instrument resting." The teacher assigns teams of four, establishes the groups who are "honks," "rattles," "crashes," and "beeps," allows the students to explore sounds, and times them to form their seated groups.

3. "Rest your instruments on the floor, please. I'll quickly count off who is partner number 1, 2, 3, and 4 in your group. [The teacher assigns a partner number for each child.] Partners 1, take your instrument and get ready to play either your honk, rattle, crash, or beep. If you are not playing, your job is to decide if the instrument is high or low, so listen carefully. I'll play the recording. Partners 1, ready and here we go." The teacher plays the recording and cues the honks, rattles, crashes, and beeps to play.

4. "Good rehearsing. You played in the right part of the song. Carefully pass your instrument to partner 2 in your group.

Partners 2, let's do the same thing. [The teacher repeats the process.] Thank you, partners 2. You handled the sounds in the right places. Please pass your instruments to partner 3 in your group. [Partners 3 play.] You played at exactly the right time. Please pass your instrument to partner 4. [Partners 4 play.] You were perfect with playing at the right time."

5. "Let's take a vote on the sounds. Partners 4, if your instrument had a high sound, would you play it until I count to three? [The teacher cues them to start and gives a large cut-off.] Partners 4, please rest your instrument on the floor. Class, if you think you heard high sounds, give me a 'thumbs up.' Yes, I'd agree. The cowbell, tambourine, and sticks have high sounds."

6. "Partners 3, if your instrument had a low sound, please play it until I count to three. [The teacher repeats the process.] I heard the Indian drum, the large hand drum, and the conga drum. Those have low sounds. You identified those correctly."

7. "Please raise your hand if you could name the instrument that best fits the honk sound. [The teacher chooses a person or two to name instruments and asks them to quickly play a few sounds in order to aurally connect the honk with a high sound.] Please raise your hand if you could name the instrument that best fits the rattle sound. [The teacher repeats the process.] The instrument most closely fitted to the crashes? [The teacher repeats the process.] And the beeps? [The teacher repeats the process.] You named instruments that had high sounds [teacher reiterates their names] and low sounds [repeats the names]."

8. "Partners 2, carefully, quickly, and quietly return your instruments to their places and sit down. Partners 1, please make sure everyone in your group is headed back to their seats."

Reading and Writing (Visual and Kinesthetic)
Materials:

- A slide with two measures of notation of the song "I Have a Car"

- Paper and markers for the class

Procedure:

1. Before class, the teacher prepares a slide of the music notation for the first two phrases of "I Have a Car" to project on the screen. The slide will focus on the iconic representation of the melody, using a line for each note at relative heights and including a connection of the lines to present the phrases. Another set of icons could then be added to show the rhythmic values, such as the long and short dashes or different-sized cars to represent quarter and eighth notes.

2. As the teacher shows the iconic presentation of the melody, he or she says, "This is what the melody or tune looks like. You will see high and low sounds that show us how the melody sounds. Notice the curve over the sounds. That curve means it is a phrase. If you know how many phrases are on the screen, show me with your fingers. [The teacher monitors the class to ensure they are holding up two fingers.] Yes, there are two."

3. "Please make your fingers follow the melody in the air while I point to the high and low sounds. I bet you can sing it with me because you already know the song. [The teacher establishes the starting pitch and cue and leads the class.] Now that you've sung and read two phrases, you get to write the last two."

4. "I have paper and markers for you. When you receive these, please rest these on the floor and wait patiently until everyone has them. It does not matter what color the marker is. You get what you get and you can handle it." The teacher has students help him or her pass out the materials.

5. "Let's see if we can figure out if the first note of the next phrase is high or low. I'll sing it and you give me a 'thumbs up' if it's high and 'thumbs down' if it's low. Yes, it's high. Please make a line to show a rather high sound at the beginning. Here's a hint. It will look like the very first line of the song because it starts the same way."

6. "I'll sing the phrase and you write the lines to show the high and low sounds of the melody. [The teacher monitors the

class's work and helps them with this task.] Let's sing the third phrase while you check your work." The teacher establishes the starting pitch and cue.

7. "Nod your head if you think your melody looks correct. Let's finish the last phrase of the song. I'll sing it while you write it. [The teacher monitors the class.] Let's check your work on the last phrase. Please sing it with me and check your work." The teacher establishes the starting pitch and cue.

8. "Please put your name on your paper, place it gently on my desk, and leave your marker in the box. You can do this and get back to your seat by the time I count to ten. One, two, three. . . . Excellent work analyzing the pitch of the notes, class."

Closure and Check of Learning

"Today we worked with the high and low sounds that make up a tune or song."

- Identification: Teacher asks a student to name something that makes a high sound and another student to name something that makes a low sound.

- Verbalization: Teacher asks the class to blurt (concerted attention to getting a group response) the new word that describes high and low sounds (*melody*).

- Demonstration: Teacher plays a melody on the keyboard while singing the accompanying solfège and asks students to show him or her each pitch on their body scales.

- Further application: Teacher asks students to find something that has a high sound or a low sound and tell the class about it in the next music class (to maintain the focus on the concept and expect accountability).

LOTS

Singing, showing the body scale, and doing the movements associated with the car sounds.

HOTS

Matching instrument sounds to car sounds and determining the highness or lowness of each sound, reading the melody iconically, and writing the melody iconically.

The Lesson Model: Grade 2

Concept: *As a part of form, phrase coupled with rhyme scheme*, threaded through every segment of this lesson

National Standards:

1. Singing, alone and with others, a varied repertoire of music.

2. Performing on instruments, alone and with others, a varied repertoire of music.

3. Composing and arranging music within specified guidelines.

4. Reading and notating music.

5. Listening to, analyzing, and describing music.

6. Understanding music in relation to history and culture.

Introduction (Visual)

Materials:

- Poster of four cars

Procedure:

1. The teacher has a large picture of four cars posted on the board, the first, second, and fourth being red and the third being yellow. He or she says, "I noticed that many of you have on blue shirts today—seven of you—and everyone else has another color. That makes me think of a pattern; everyone is dressed either in blue or not in blue. Today we are going to investigate patterns and make some of our own music with it."

2. "In a few minutes you are going to be composers, but first we have to prepare for that just like you get ready to come to school or get ready for bed. Please look at my picture of the cars. Smile

at me if you can see things that are the same about the cars and something that is different. If you could describe the pattern using the words *same* and *different*, please raise your hand." The teacher chooses a student to verbalize "same–same–different–same" or "three cars are the same and one is different."

3. "You found it! If the first car is red, is the second one the same or different? Please blurt the answer. [The class blurts.] Is the third one the same or different? Please blurt the answer . . . and what about the last one? Please blurt again. . . . Hmm." As the teacher points to the respective cars, he or she says, "You've noticed that the pattern is 'same–same–different–same.' We're going to use that pattern today. Please close your eyes and see the pattern of the cars in your mind. You'll need to remember the pattern."

Moving (Auditory, Visual, and Kinesthetic)
Materials:

- The "Honey, You Can't Love One" song for the teacher

Procedure:

1. The teacher prepares to teach the song "Honey, You Can't Love One" (traditional). "Please get your ears ready to listen and your bodies resting. [Teacher makes sure the class is ready for this before proceeding.] I'm going to speak the first phrase or thought in the music. Please listen to it [teacher speaks the first phrase, 'Honey, you can't love one']. Now listen to the next phrase or thought and see if it is the same as the first one or different." The teacher speaks the second phrase, "Honey, you can't love one."

2. "Please give me a 'thumbs up' if the phrases were the same or a 'thumbs down' if they were different. Yes! You noticed it correctly. They were the *same*. Now listen to the third phrase or thought and show me with your thumbs. ['You can't love one and still have your fun.'] Correct. You noticed it was *different*. And here's the last one. You know what to do. ['Oh, honey, you can't love one.'] It's the *same*. You were correct with all four phrases of the song. Good work!"

3. "In a moment you are going to move around the room in a kind of game. Let me show you what we'll be doing. When I sing the first phrase, you will walk to the beat in one direction [teacher demonstrates a few steps in one direction]. When I sing the second phrase, you will walk to the beat in the same direction [teacher continues in the same direction]. On the third phrase, you will change your direction to show that it's different [teacher changes direction]. And on the last phrase you will walk in the same direction as the first two phrases." The teacher shows the initial direction.

4. "There are only two things we must remember to do: keep our feet on the floor and avoid touching anybody or anything. Please show me that you can handle that so that everyone can stay in this game. Without any fussing, please stand up in your own hula hoop space and get ready to move in one direction with walking feet. Rea-dy and here we go."

5. The teacher sings the first phrase, pausing at the end of it, then proceeds through the second phrase, pausing again; he or she sings the third phrase, emphasizing vocally that it is different and pausing at its end, then finishes the last phrase and gives the cut-off or stopping cue to the class. "Please move back to your seats on the beat while I sing the song softly."

Singing (Auditory, Visual, and Kinesthetic)
Materials:

- The "Honey, You Can't Love One" song for the teacher

Procedure:

1. "Please get your posture ready to sing the song. [The teacher checks the class for upright body positions.] I will sing a phrase to you and you sing it back to me. [The teacher models each phrase, then gives the starting pitch and cues the class to echo him or her.] Let's sing the entire first verse together." The teacher sings with the class.

2. "I'm going to give the first phrase an easy name to remember. I'll call it 'A.' Please sing the first phrase to me. [The teacher establishes the starting pitch and cues the class to sing it, cutting them off at the end of the phrase.] That was 'A.' Boys, please sing the second phrase. [The teacher gives the starting pitch and cues them.] If you believe that is similar to the first phrase, give me a 'thumbs up.' Yes, it is."

3. "So we will need to give this phrase a name. Melanie, what do you think we should call it? I believe you are correct. It is A again. Girls, please sing the third phrase. [The teacher gives the starting pitch and cue.] Jesus, is that the same as A or is it different? Excellent answer. You knew it was different."

4. "Hmmm. If we called the first two phrases A, what should we call this one, Bill? [The teacher will need to dignify any response that is different from 'A'—for example, 'double M' or 'Z'.] I like your choice of B. It's different from A. Everyone, sing the last phrase with me. Let's see if it's similar to A or to B." The teacher gives the pitch and cue.

5. "As we sing the song together, could you use your 'invisible pen' to write the letter A in the air during the A phrases? Let's practice it. I'll sing the first phrase and you write an A. [The class practices.] Let's try the B phrase. I'll sing and you write. [The class practices.] You are ready to do it on your own. [The teacher gives the pitch and cue; the class sings and writes.] You were right on in determining the A and B phrases, showing the pattern AABA. Very accurate listening, class."

Performing (Auditory and Kinesthetic)
Materials:

- Unpitched percussion instruments for the class

- Piano or other keyboard

Procedure:

1. The teacher prepares the class for performance, focusing on the rhythm in the song to reinforce the words' durations.

"We're going to play percussion instruments, so you'll need to remember how we do this. Let me refresh your memory. I will walk over to the instruments [teacher walks to the shelf], choose one [he or she selects one], and carry it back to my seat without noise [he or she models this]. The instrument will rest until everyone is ready to play."

2. "Row 3, please do that and show the class how it's done [that row gets instruments]. Row 2, please do it just like row 3 did it. They have handled the instruments carefully and without noise. Row 1, you know what to do [they get instruments]. Thank you for handling the instruments with care. I appreciate your waiting patiently for everyone to get them."

3. "Girls, you will play the rhythm of the words during A phrases, and boys, you will do it during the B phrase. I'll play the song on the piano. Everyone, get your instruments ready. Girls, ready, here you go. [The teacher cues the boys to play during their phrase, then switches the assignment in which the boys play A and girls play B.] Everyone, play the rhythm of the words for the entire verse. One, two, rea-dy, play. [The class plays the first verse.] Thank you for paying attention to the words' rhythm. You were very accurate with that."

4. "Please get your instruments ready to be put away. Row 1, please return yours to the shelf without noise and then wait patiently in your chairs. Row 2, please do the same. Row 3, you know what to do. . . . Thank you for doing that quickly and carefully. Now comes the good stuff. You are going to be composers."

Reading and Writing; Improvising, Composing, and Creating (Visual, Auditory, and Kinesthetic)
Materials:

• Whiteboard, marker, and eraser

Procedure:

1. The teacher prepares the class: "Please sing the first phrase in your head and blurt the last word. [The teacher writes the word

one on the board.] Now do the same with the second phrase [he or she writes *one* on the board]. Here comes the third phrase. You know what to do [he or she writes *fun* on the board]. And finally, the last phrase [*one*]. Here is our AABA pattern."

2. "Look what happened in the song. It says, 'Honey, you can't love *one*. . . . Honey, you can't love *one*. . . . You can't love one and still have your *fun*. . . . Oh, honey, you can't love *one*.' Rub your knee if you notice something about those words. Serena, what did you notice? Yes, they rhyme. There's a number, the same number, a rhyming word with it, and the same number again, but everything rhymes."

3. "There is another verse that uses the number two. Let's read it and see what word rhymes with *two*. [The teacher asks four students to read the phrases and he or she writes the 'two–two–true–two' pattern on the board.] Let's sing the second verse. [He or she establishes the starting pitch and cue.] You read the words very well."

4. "Let's see about the third verse. Now that you know the pattern, we could probably predict that a certain number will occur three times. Touch your nose if you know the number. Giles, what is that number? Yes, it is three. So there are three *threes* in the pattern." The teacher writes the "three–three–_____–three" pattern on the board.

5. "Our job is to compose our own words. We'll sing 'You can't love three and . . .' then we fill in the next part. It has a *ti ta ti ta* rhythm. Let's clap it. Ready, and here we go." The class claps *ti ta ti ta*.

6. "Raise your hand if you can think of the rest of the words that would follow 'You can't love three and . . .' This is where the *ti ta ti ta* is. [Examples might be 'You can't love three and still go with me' or 'You can't love three and sit on my knee.'] I like your choice, Sedra. [The teacher writes the rhyming word in the pattern.] Let's sing the third verse with our new words." Pitch and cue are given.

7. "Let's try one more verse. If our number is four and we need the *ti ta ti ta* pattern, who could compose new words to complete this

verse? Wave your pinkie if you can do this. [The teacher writes the four–four–_____–four pattern on the board. A choice might be 'You can't love four and love anymore.'] Excellent rhyming word, Petra. Everyone, sing the fourth verse with me [teacher gives pitch and cue]. Wonderful composing, class. You did exactly the right number of words to fit the *ti ta ti ta* rhythm."

Listening (Auditory and Visual)
Materials:

- Recording of "Trepak" from *The Nutcracker Suite*

- World map or globe

- Posters of the string family

Procedure:

1. This piece is from *The Nutcracker Suite* (Silver-Burdett, 2005, has a listening map in the third-grade text that has AABA form). "You are so good at finding the pattern that we'll finish with one of my favorite pieces of music, which was written way back in 1891 by a Russian composer named Pyotr Ilyich Tchaikovsky." The teacher shows a picture of him.

2. "Russia is a country across the ocean and here is where it is located on our big map [the teacher points to it]. Here is where we live [teacher points], so notice how far away it is. The piece is called 'Trepak,' which means 'Russian dance.' You will hear a large orchestra play this and you'll notice the violins, violas, cellos, and basses [teacher shows pictures of each]. Please put your eyes on the listening map and get your bodies ready. When we're done listening, please tell me what the pattern of the music is. The hint is that you can use letters that we used today."

3. The teacher projects the map and the class listens, noting the AABA pattern. "Please give a 'thumbs up' if you know the pattern of the letters of this music. Yukiko, please tell the class what you think the pattern is. [She said AABA.] If you agree with her, clap your hands four times. If you disagree, tap your

toes. Exactly! It's AABA, just like our song. You identified the pattern the first time you listened to the music. That is amazing, second grade. Thank you for being such good detectives in discovering the pattern."

Closure and Check of Learning
"Today we learned more about a particular pattern in music."

- Verbalization: Teacher asks a student to tell the class the pattern with the appropriate letters.

- Identification: Teacher asks someone to go to the car poster and point to the part of the pattern that is different from the rest of the pattern.

- Demonstration: Teacher asks the class to sing the B pattern in the song at the appropriate time (he or she sings A and lets them "fill in" the B segment).

- Further application: Teacher asks the students to listen to their favorite music at home and see if it has an AABA pattern (to maintain the focus on the concept and expect accountability).

LOTS
Singing the song as a group, and playing the rhythm of the words on instruments.

HOTS
Reading the words of the song and the rhyming pattern, then creating and identifying the pattern in listening.

The Lesson Model: Grade 3
Concept: *Dynamics*, threaded through every segment of this lesson
National Standards:

1. Singing, alone and with others, a varied repertoire of music.

2. Performing on instruments, alone and with others, a varied repertoire of music.

3. Improvising melodies, variations, and accompaniments.

4. Reading and notating music.

5. Listening to, analyzing, and describing music.

6. Understanding music in relation to history and culture.

Singing (Visual and Auditory)
Materials:

- A slide of the song "Deaf Woman's Courtship"

- Pictures of sheep and a spinning wheel

- Flashcards, one with *f* on it and one with *p*

Procedure:

1. The teacher begins by asking the class if they have ever heard or read a story about someone who was playing a trick. He or she gives them a moment to respond and then proceeds. "Today I have a neat song in which there are two people, one of whom is playing a trick. Let me show you the song. Since this is an old song, there are some words in it that are probably new to you."

2. "Picture yourself living on a farm and raising a lot of sheep. Here is a picture of sheep and you'll notice their fluffy coats [teacher shows picture]. Do you know what material we use that comes from sheep? Yes, it is wool. When the wool is shaved off the sheep, it is cleaned and untangled, and that's called 'carding.' Next the carded wool is spun using a spinning wheel [teacher shows a picture of it] to make yarn and that yarn can then be woven into fabric for clothes or knitted into sweaters and socks."

3. "Please look at 'The Deaf Woman's Courtship' [traditional song] and remember that the woman supposedly cannot hear. A courtship means someone is dating someone else. In this song, there is an old woman and a young man. Let's prepare to listen. Your ears are open and mouths are resting [teacher

scans class to ensure they are ready]. Listen quietly to the entire song. When you know what the trick is, give me a silent
signal, a 'thumbs up.'" The teacher presents the song on the
screen and sings it for the class, gradually singing the man's
part softer and the woman's part louder.

4. "Let me ask one person to share what the trick is. [The teacher
selects a child to discuss this, gently accepting responses that
may not be quite correct and acknowledging that the children
offered answers.] Yes, the trick is that the woman tries to
convince the man that she cannot hear until he proposes to
her, but she has been able to hear all the way along. Very good
listening, class, for you figured it out without help from me.
You listened carefully. Thank you."

5. "I have a new sign to show you [he or she shows a card with
the forte (f) symbol on it]. Watch what happens when the
word *forte* tells me how to sing this. [The teacher demonstrates
singing the man's first two lines of song at the forte level.]
What did you notice? Amy, what do you think *forte* means?
You are correct. It means 'loud.'"

6. "Another sign says *piano* [teacher shows the sign with p on
it] and I'll sing the woman's line now. [The teacher sings her
line at the piano level.] Class, please blurt this answer. If forte
means loud, piano then means. . . . You are absolutely correct.
It means 'soft.' I will show you the signs and we'll try the song
using forte and piano, but you must remember that forte does
not mean to use a yelling voice. It's a louder voice than piano,
but it's never a yelling one."

7. The teacher proceeds with establishing the starting pitch, giving
the starting cue, reviewing the song, and indicating the dynamics
for forte and piano throughout and having the class perform.

Performing (Auditory)
Materials:

- Piano or other keyboard

- A slide of the song "Deaf Woman's Courtship"

Procedure:

1. "Now that you've learned piano and forte, let's add a bit of drama to this story. Men, please sing the first two lines of every verse, starting with forte and gradually becoming piano by the last verse. Women, you will do the *opposite* by singing only the last line of every verse, starting with piano and gradually becoming forte by the last verse."

2. The teacher establishes the starting pitch, cues them to begin, and allows them to perform. He or she physically cues them on each so that the boys gradually use diminuendo and the girls crescendo.

Moving (Auditory, Visual, and Kinesthetic)
Materials:

- Flashcard with the word *dynamics* on it

Procedure:

1. "Since you have sung and performed both piano and forte sounds, I'm going to give you the name that means both loud and soft in music. It is *dynamics*. [Teacher presents the word on a sign.] Say the word with me, please. [The class speaks the word.] We are going to use dynamics to play rhythm with our bodies."

2. "I will either clap [teacher demonstrates a four-beat pattern], snap [teacher demonstrates a four-beat pattern], patsch [teacher demonstrates], or stomp [teacher demonstrates] using body percussion. I will play a pattern and then you will echo me. Ready and here I go."

3. The teacher plays simple patterns with clapping and the class echoes; he or she repeats them, adding dynamics. He or she continues with various patterns, ultimately blending clapping, snapping, patsching, and stomping with dynamic changes.

4. "Excellent playing, class. You listened closely and remembered the pattern and the dynamics. Now you're going to get to listen to an entire orchestra use dynamics in one of my favorite pieces of music."

Listening (Visual and Auditory)
Materials:

- Picture of Franz Haydn
- World map or globe
- Recording of Haydn's *Surprise Symphony* (second movement)

Procedure:

1. "Please look at the picture of the man who wrote or composed this music. His name is Franz Joseph Haydn and he lived across the ocean in a country called Austria." Teacher shows Austria on a map or globe and then trances a straight line back to the location of the class's town or city.

2. "He wrote many pieces of music, but wanted to surprise his audience with something that was new and different. The piece we will hear is called the *Surprise Symphony* and it was written in the year 1791, which is around 220 years ago."

3. "Because you are the audience, you will be prepared to handle his surprise with only a smile. Here is what will happen. The music will be piano—gentle and soft—then becoming softer. Suddenly there is a loud chord that you will hear. I know you are mature enough to handle this only by smiling, so let's rehearse it."

4. The teacher goes to the keyboard and plays gently, then prepares the class to hear a loud chord. "Thank you for smiling when you heard it. I appreciate your mature behavior. You are ready for the real thing. When we're done, I will ask you what happened *after* the loud chord. Did the music remain forte or did it become piano? Please don't blurt, just wait for me to ask. Show me you're ready for listening. Your ears are open, mouths are resting, and you are awaiting the music. Thank you."

5. The teacher plays roughly one-and-a-half to two minutes of the piece's second movement, monitoring the class to ensure they are practicing audience behavior. "I saw lots of smiles

when the loud chord was played. Wave at me if you know what the music did after the chord. Was it piano or forte?" Teacher asks a student to identify the dynamic level. "Yes, it became mostly piano after that. I loved the way you handled the loud chord. Thank you for being so mature with the listening."

Reading and Writing (Auditory, Visual, and Kinesthetic)
Materials:

- Whiteboards, markers, and erasers for the class

- The songs "Jingle Bells," "America," "Rudolph, the Red-Nosed Reindeer," "Mary Had a Little Lamb," and "Row, Row, Row Your Boat" for the teacher

Procedure:

1. "Now that you can hear the dynamics with your ears, we get to practice writing dynamics. When you get a whiteboard, please lay it on your lap and wait patiently for a marker and an eraser."

2. The teacher has students pass out the equipment and then speaks softly. "Let's pretend that we are listening to 'Jingle Bells' [Pierpont, written in 1857] on the keyboard and it's very gentle. We would write a *p* for *piano*. Please practice writing one on your board."

3. Teacher writes this on the board, asks the class to do it also, and then speaks with more volume. "Then the next piece is a loud version of 'America' [lyrics written by Smith in 1831]. We will want to write a fancy *f* for *forte*. Please write that on your board, too."

4. The teacher demonstrates, has the class practice, and then speaks at a moderate volume. "Erase your boards and let's try this without my clues. I'll play a bit of a song and you write either *p* or *f*, and then I'll ask you to show me your boards. Here we go."

5. The teacher plays bits of familiar songs such as "Rudolph, the Red-Nosed Reindeer" (Marks, 1949), "Mary Had a Little Lamb" (traditional song), and "Row, Row, Row Your Boat" (traditional song), demonstrating soft dynamics on two pieces and loud on the others.

6. The students show their boards after each song and the teacher quickly scans to ensure everyone is responding correctly. If not, he or she stops to demonstrate piano and forte levels of the same song and retries the example. "You were very accurate with identifying the dynamics for the pieces. I am so proud of you for listening and writing accurately and without noise."

Improvising, Composing, and Creating (Auditory, Visual, and Kinesthetic)
Materials:

- Recorders for the class and the teacher

- The *Quick as a Cricket* book

Procedure:

1. This part of the lesson assumes that the class has had some introductory instruction on recorders prior to this lesson. "You have sung, listened, and played dynamics today, but now you get to create them. I have my recorder to remind you how to hold it [teacher demonstrates] and how to blow without squeaking [teacher demonstrates]. In a moment you will each have one and you'll be able to use the one note that we know, which is B." The teacher demonstrates.

2. "The book that I have is called *Quick as a Cricket* [Wood, 1992] and you'll see things like this. [The teacher opens to the first picture, that of a cricket.] After I read the line about the cricket, you will have four beats to make *quick* sounds on your recorder. For instance, it might sound like this." The teacher reads the line, plays quick sounds on the recorder on the note B for four seconds, and stops.

3. "The next page is devoted to a slow snail. You'll have four counts to make *slow-w-w-w* sounds. Listen to four seconds of slow sounds. [The teacher demonstrates on B.] I will pass out the recorders and you will tuck them under your arms to wait until we begin to play together."

4. The teacher hands out recorders and instructs students to place them under their arms in "pit position" until everyone has one. "Please take them out and let's practice. Make sure you are holding the recorder properly [teacher scans them to ensure positions are accurate], prepare your lips over your teeth for the correct embouchure, then play B without squeaking [he or she cues them to play B and then cuts them off], and now you're ready to do it without me."

5. The teacher reads a line, says "rea-dy, go" or physically cues them to begin, and counts to four with his or her fingers before cutting them off and moving to the next page; he or she proceeds through the book, focusing on the adjectives for each line and cueing the class to perform for four counts each.

6. "We are now finished, so place them back under your arms. Thank you for such wonderful sounds! You listened so well and made very appropriate sounds on your recorders. Trisha, please give a paper towel to each person and I will spray disinfectant on your mouthpiece. Make sure you're not breathing on it. Clean it thoroughly, then deposit your paper towel in the trash, your recorder in the box, and yourself back in your seat. Let's see if we can complete this in less than a minute. John, please watch the clock for me and tell me when a minute has passed." The class proceeds with cleaning and storing the recorders before closure occurs.

Closure and Check of Learning
"Today we learned three new words that describe sounds."

- Verbalization: Teacher asks a student to share the word that means louds and softs in music with the class (*dynamics*); another to name the word that designates soft sounds (*piano*); and a third to verbalize the word for loud (*forte*).

- Identification: Teacher asks the class to use "invisible ink" to write the letters that mean soft (*p*) and loud (*f*) in the air.

- Demonstration: Teacher asks the class to whisper "piano" when he or she plays a soft phrase on the keyboard and blurt "forte" after hearing a loud one.

- Further application: Teacher asks the students to listen to their favorite music at home and determine if the song has dynamics (to maintain the focus on the concept and expect accountability).

LOTS

Singing the song as a group, recognizing the dynamic levels, and performing with body percussion and recorders.

HOTS

Creating the dynamics and identifying the significance of the trick and its use of dynamics in the song.

The Lesson Model: Grade 3

Concept: *Tempo as related to rhythm*, threaded through every segment of this lesson

National Standards:

1. Singing, alone and with others, a varied repertoire of music.

2. Performing on instruments, alone and with others, a varied repertoire of music.

3. Improvising melodies, variations, and accompaniments.

4. Reading and notating music.

5. Listening to, analyzing, and describing music.

6. Understanding music in relation to history and culture.

Performing (Visual, Auditory, and Kinesthetic)
Materials:

- Flashcard with the word *tempo* on it

Procedure:

1. "Today we are going to experiment with the word *tempo*. If I walk across the room at this tempo [teacher demonstrates very slowly] and then I walk back at this tempo [teacher walks back at a fast tempo], I have changed something. If you know what it is, please pat your knees." Teacher asks a student to identify that the speed changed.

2. "Exactly. I changed my speed. The music word for speed is *tempo* [the teacher shows a card with the vocabulary word on it]. Please say the word with me. Tem-po."

3. "Let's practice some body percussion. I'll clap, snap, or patsch a pattern to you and you'll echo it back to me. Let me start with a slow tempo." The teacher claps a four-beat pattern slowly to the class and they echo it. He or she proceeds through four or five different patterns, gradually speeding up.

4. "We changed our tempo. Some music does that. But other music carefully takes just one tempo throughout. Let's try a few more patterns to see if we can keep a *steady* tempo." The teacher presents three more patterns and the class echoes these.

5. "Today you will be tempo detectives, so let's put on our investigator's hats and get our spyglasses out to look closely at tempo [the teacher pantomimes this through body movements]. Let's get to work."

Singing (Auditory)
Materials:

- Slide of "There Are Many Flags in Many Lands" song
- Projector and screen
- Piano or other keyboard

Procedure:

1. "Last time we met we learned the song 'There Are Many Flags in Many Lands' [composer unknown, text by Mary H.

Howliston]. Today we are going to play with the tempo. Please carefully and quietly look at the song on the screen. Get your bodies in singing position and follow me. We'll begin by singing it rather slowly." The teacher establishes the starting pitch, cues the class to sing, and accompanies them.

2. "You stayed exactly in a *steady* tempo with me, but I'm so curious to see if you can follow my *changes* in tempo. Let's try it again. Please get positioned to sing." The teacher establishes the starting pitch and cues the students to sing, accompanying them with gradual faster changes in the song's tempo.

3. "Hmmm. You followed extremely well. But I'm still wondering if you can follow *both* slow and fast changes. One more time to try it out [the teacher establishes the pitch and cue, but this time does obvious, gradual changes to slow the tempo and to speed it up]. I'm amazed that you are such excellent listeners. You followed the changes well and stayed right with me as we sped up and slowed down. Thank you."

Listening (Auditory and Kinesthetic)
Materials:

- Recording of Mosolov's *Symphony of Machines, Steel Foundry*

Procedure:

1. The teacher prepares to plays a recording of Mosolov's *Symphony of Machines, Steel Foundry* (sometime referred to as the *Iron Foundry*, written in 1926–1927), and in this instance, he or she does not share its title or composer.

2. "My favorite part is finally here. I have a very unusual piece of music to play for you. Please imagine that you were working in a factory and your job was to help build a car or a tractor. You might be among many machines that were all working at the same time. It might even be quite noisy. Please get your ears ready for listening, for you'll need to investigate whether the machines you hear—which are actually instruments in the

orchestra trying to imitate machines—are working at different tempos or if they're working with one steady tempo. As we listen, you can give me a hint that you know by tapping one finger on your knee if you determine there is only one tempo. If you find only one tempo, play it on your knee. Ears are open, mouths are resting, and you're quiet and ready to hear the music."

3. The teacher scans the class to ensure they are ready to listen, then plays approximately a minute or so of the piece, scanning the class to see if they've responded to the tempo. "Megan, what do you know about the tempo of that music? Yes, it is very steady and does not change. I noticed you found the tempo and tapped it."

4. "Please listen once more and find the tempo again with your finger on your knee. Our goal is to see if everyone can determine the steady tempo [the teacher plays it again and scans the class to see if they have correctly identified it]. You found it! Accurate listening, class. The tempo is extremely steady, never getting faster or slower. So today we're going to make our own factory and imitate that steady tempo."

Improvising, Composing, and Creating; Moving (Auditory, Visual, and Kinesthetic)
Materials: None

Procedure:

1. "In a moment, we are going to create our own factory. That factory is going to be a pickle factory and it will include everything from harvesting the cucumbers from the garden to loading the boxes of pickle jars on the truck to travel to the grocery store. Each of you will be your own machine and will be a part of the process of making the pickles."

2. "Each of you will need to invent a movement to show your machine and then add an appropriate sound to match it. For instance, if I am the farmer harvesting the cucumbers from the garden, I would reach down to get the cucumber, turn and put

it in a basket, and then repeat the process. My movement might be like this." The teacher demonstrates picking the cucumbers from the ground and throwing them in the bushel basket, making a sound for reaching and another for dropping them.

3. "Let's pretend that the cucumbers have been loaded on a truck and delivered to the factory. Here is where your job begins. Mia, please start our factory by standing near the door. You are to run the long conveyer belt that takes the baskets of cucumbers into the factory. Please invent a movement and a sound to repeat over and over until the entire factory is at work."

4. The teacher may need to help the first few students with their improvisations. "As Mia continues, Neil, please dump the cucumbers from the boxes into a huge sink to wash them." Neil invents his movement and sound; the teacher continues to establish specific jobs for everyone, doubling people into jobs if necessary so that everyone is involved.

5. "Alli, the next one is spraying the water on the cukes and washing them. Jesus, you will dump the washed cucumbers onto another belt to dry them."

6. The teacher continues with a dryer, a slicer, a furnace to make the glass jars, a steel roll to make the jar lids, a large roll of paper to print the jar labels, a paster to apply the labels, a machine to slice the cucumbers and then insert them into the jars, an injector to add a mixture of vinegar, water, and spices for the pickles, an applier for the lids, a jar washer, a machine to box the jars, a sealer for the boxes, a loader onto the truck, and so forth.

7. "Now that everyone is making their movements, let's make sure we're all working at the same tempo [the teacher establishes the tempo if necessary, saying 'move and repeat, move and repeat,' allowing them to work for thirty seconds]. It's nearly five o'clock and time for the factory to begin to shut down. Let's slowly change our tempo and get . . . rea-dy . . . to . . . stop." The teacher pantomimes blowing a whistle to designate quitting time.

8. "It's time for everyone to move back to your seats. You had a wonderful steady tempo until we began to shut down. I wonder what would happen if the washer went faster than the slicer, or the lids were made more slowly than the jars. Could you predict what would happen in our factory?"

9. The teacher asks them to comment on this and determine that different tempos would not allow the factory to work successfully. "You figured it out. Excellent predictions. And that is exactly why musicians must sing or play instruments at the same tempo. If they did not do that, the music would sound like a mess."

Reading and Writing (Auditory, Visual, and Kinesthetic)
Materials:

- Flashcard with the word *andante* on it

- Flashcard with the word *allegro* on it

- Slide of "There Are Many Flags in Many Lands" song

- The song "America" for the class

- Projector and screen

Procedure:

1. "To finish today I have two music words to show you that are related to the word *tempo*. If I use a rather slow walking tempo to sing 'There Are Many Flags in Many Lands,' the fancy Italian word is *andante* [the teacher shows a card with the new word on it]. Say it with me, please. An-dan-te. *Andante* means a slow walking tempo."

2. "Tapping your toes on the floor, let's find an andante tempo [the teacher helps them to establish a steady slow tempo]. Let's sing our song with that tempo." He or she establishes the pitch and cues and they sing.

3. "If I want to go faster, I need another fancy Italian word such as *allegro* [teacher shows another card with the word on it].

Please say it with me. Al-le-gro. *Allegro* means a fast-running tempo. Let's sing the song with an allegro tempo." Teacher establishes pitch and cues and they sing.

4. "I'll ask you to make another prediction. When you are ready to share it with the class, wave to me. Which tempo do you think is more appropriate for the song and why do you think that?" The teacher asks a few students to offer answers and justification, anticipating that they'll argue for both tempos.

5. "So it could be slow in order to understand the words? Or it could be fast to make it more appealing? I think you are very correct. Your reasons were good ones. Now you are ready to write the tempo marking on another song."

6. "I will give you a sheet with a song called 'America,' which you learned in second grade. Nod your head if you remember this. [The teacher hums just a few measures of this.] Joel will give you a pencil. Please sing the song *in your head* and then write the correct tempo marking under the song's title. You have one minute to do this. Please rest your pencil when you're finished." The teacher monitors this.

7. "Now that you've marked the tempo, Janna, tell what the tempo should be. Yes, andante is probably the best choice. Let's sing it at an andante tempo." The teacher gives the starting pitch and cue and the class sings it.

8. "Just so we can make a comparison, let's try singing it with an allegro tempo. [The teacher establishes pitch and cue again.] Bill, did that work well for that song? Josie, why not? Correct. It was difficult to read the words that fast. And perhaps if it's tough to read the words, it's even more difficult to understand them if you're listening to the song. Excellent comparison, class." The teacher has the students pass in their papers and collects their pencils before beginning closure.

Closure and Check of Learning

"Today we worked with words that described something about the speed of the music."

- Verbalization: Teacher asks a student to share the word that means fast speed (*allegro*), another to name the word that designates slow speed (*andante*), and a third to verbalize the word for speed in music (*tempo*).

- Identification: Teacher asks the class to give a "thumbs up" if the music is fast and a "thumbs down" if it is slow (he or she plays fifteen seconds of "Happy Birthday" at a very slow speed in order to use a calming end to the lesson).

- Demonstration: Teacher asks the class to tap the steady tempo as he or she plays thirty seconds of the *Symphony of Machines*.

- Further application: Teacher asks the students to listen to their favorite music at home and determine if the song has a steady tempo or a changing tempo (to maintain the focus on the concept and expect accountability).

LOTS

Echoing the body percussion, singing the song with different tempos, and playing the beat of the music.

HOTS

Creating their own movements and sounds in accordance with a steady tempo for the "machines," and comparing tempos in the music justifying the responses.

The Lesson Model: Grade 4

Concept: *Rhythm (triplets)*, threaded through every segment of this lesson

National Standards:

1. Singing, alone and with others, a varied repertoire of music.

2. Performing on instruments, alone and with others, a varied repertoire of music.

3. Improvising melodies, variations, and accompaniments.

4. Reading and notating music.

5. Listening to, analyzing, and describing music.

6. Understanding music in relation to history and culture.

Introduction (Auditory and Visual)
Materials:

- Flashcard with iconic rhythm (three equal dashes)

- Flashcard with the word *trip-o-let* on it

Procedure:

1. "Fourth grade, we are going to learn a snazzy rhythm today that is represented in the word *rasp-ber-ry* [each syllable evenly stressed]. Repeat after me." The teacher says "rasp-ber-ry," and the class echoes it.

2. "If I make a picture of the rhythm, it looks like this [a flashcard with three equal dashes: — — —]. Watch me point to the picture while you say the word *rasp-ber-ry*." Teacher points to each dash noting the syllables of the word.

3. "I can remember the rhythm with the word *trip-o-let* [showing another flashcard with the three dashes and the *trip-o-let* word written below it]. Please say that word with me. Trip-o-let. I added the *o* in the middle of *trip-o-let* to show it with three sounds like *rasp-ber-ry*. The real word is *triplet*. If I want to read the music of the triplet, it looks like this [shows another flashcard with the triplet notated in eighth notes]. Today we're going to make music with triplets."

Performing (Auditory and Kinesthetic)
Materials:

- Piano or other keyboard

Procedure:

1. "I'm going to move to the piano and I will play a steady beat [he or she plays obvious chords of steady beats in 3/4 time]. Now I'll change to triplets [plays triplet examples]. While I play steady beats, please clap triplets against the steady beat [teacher and class play and without stopping] and now switch to steady beat while I play triplets [they continue with the teacher signaling switches between beat and triplets a few times until the class performs without problems]. You are ready to listen for them in a wonderful piece of music I found."

Listening (Auditory)
Materials:

- Recording of Bizet's *Carillon*

- World map or globe

- A picture of Georges Bizet

- A picture of a campanile

- Piano or other keyboard

Procedure:

1. "You've just practiced steady beat and triplets in clapping each of these, but now you'll hear examples of each in the music. Listen to just a little bit of the beginning of this piece and you'll hear the steady beats." The teacher plays a few measures of a recording of *Carillon* (Bizet, written in 1872), indicating the first triplet by holding up the triplet rhythm card when it occurs, knowing that the piece is in 3/4 time.

2. "What you need to know about this piece is that it was written by a French composer [teacher points to France on a map or globe, then traces the path to the school's location] whose name was Bizet [teacher shows a picture of the composer], who was born in France in 1838, and was composing and reading music by the time he was only four years old. The piece we're going to hear is named *Carillon* and it was written to

portray the bells that are played in a campanile." The teacher shows a picture of a campanile.

3. "I'll play an excerpt or portion of this. Your job is to prepare to be quiet listeners, so please get your ears ready and let your lips rest. You'll hear the steady beats in the beginning, but then the triplets will occur. When you hear a triplet, please wave to me." Teacher plays the example, helping the class identify the triplets in the beginning and then gradually backing away so they can do it on their own. He or she plays approximately one-and-a-half to two minutes of the piece. "Excellent listening, class. You found the triplets! You now know how to perform and hear them. You are ready for reading them and then creating your own rhythm with them."

Singing (Auditory and Visual)
Materials:

- Slide of the "One Bottle of Pop" song

- Projector and screen

- Piano or other keyboard

Procedure:

1. The teacher shows the music on an overhead or projects it on a PowerPoint slide so that he or she can point to each note as the class learns to sight-read the song. "Please look at the music for a song called 'One Bottle of Pop' [traditional piece] that shows quarter notes and triplets. Look closely and you'll notice there are only two pitches in the song. You know how to read those, so please touch your knee if you recall the notes' names." The teacher asks one student to identify E, and another, B.

2. "On the piano here's what E sounds like [plays it]. If we begin on E and *count down* to B, what is the distance between the two notes, class? Please blurt the answer. Yes, it is a fourth. I'll play E again. In your head sing down a fourth to B and sing it out loud. [The teacher plays E, then cues with hand levels for them to silently sing D and C before singing B out loud.]

You did it! I'm going to play the E, then sing the first phrase, 'one bot-tle of pop, two bot-tles of pop,' and you will think the pitches in your head between E and B. You'll then sing 'three bot-tles of pop' on B. Let's try that much."

3. The teacher gives him- or herself the starting pitch and sings the first two measures of the song, cueing the students to enter on and sing the third measure. The teacher proceeds with this, modeling the "four bottles of pop, five bottles of pop, six bottles of pop" on E and then stopping to show the class the unusual sixteenth note and dotted eighth on B. He or she models this on B and then finishes on E with "pop."

4. "Let's do the entire song. I'll sing the Es and you sing the Bs. [The teacher establishes the starting pitch and then begins the song on E with the class singing the Bs.] This time, let's switch. Here's your starting pitch." He or she gives the starting pitch and the class performs the Es while he or she sings the Bs.

5. "You were very accurate on the Bs, matching the pitch each time you sang it. Wow, I think you're ready to do the entire song without me. [He or she gives the starting pitch and they sing the entire song.] You matched the Es and Bs right on pitch. Your rhythm was accurate, especially on the triplets. Good reading, class."

6. "Let's sing it once more and speed up the tempo a bit. [The teacher gives the starting pitch and cue in a slightly faster tempo; the class sings without the teacher. If there are mismatched rhythms or pitches, the teacher repairs these and then reviews the song again.] We're going to create a piece that has three different sections to it. The song is our first section and I bet you remember that we call that the A section. We'll use our bodies to create a *different* section called B."

Moving (Visual and Kinesthetic)
Materials: None

Procedure:

1. "Please stand in front of your chairs in your own personal space. We are going to use our bodies to create a triplet pattern. I'll

show you one and then you can create your own. Mine is clapping once and then tapping each leg [teacher models the three movements matching the triplet as clap, tap, tap]. I can do it and say 'trip-o-let' each time I perform it. Try it with me. One, rea-dy, clap." The teacher has the class do this four times and then cues the class to cut off.

2. "You just performed four triplets in a row. You now have thirty seconds to create your own pattern in which you show three *appropriate* movements in the same order each time to play four triplets in a row. The rules are that you cannot touch anybody or anything. Rea-dy and go." Teacher times them; if they appear to finish before the thirty seconds, he or she cues them to stop; he or she watches the clock and cuts them off after thirty seconds.

3. "Let's try your triplets all together. You will all perform it four times and then stop with me. Rea-dy and here you go! [The teacher holds up one finger to show one triplet, two for two, and so on to four, and then cuts them off.] Freeze there."

4. "Let's have row 3 perform theirs while everyone else watches with good audience manners. Row 3, please perform your triplets four times, then row 2 does theirs, and finally, row 1. We have four patterns times three rows, so there will be twelve patterns to watch and listen. One, rea-dy, go." Teacher cues each row to begin.

5. "You started and stopped right with me. Good musicianship, fourth grade. Your patterns were very inventive. Do remember your pattern for you'll use it later in the lesson. Think it in your head once more so that you remember it. What you just did was our B section."

Reading and Writing; Improvising, Composing, and Creating (Auditory, Visual, and Kinesthetic)
Materials:

- Sets of rhythm cards for each group of four to five students

Procedure:

1. "For the third or C section, you are going to have rhythm cards. Each card has one rhythmic element on it. For example, here is the card with the quarter note. Everyone clap it with me. Rea-dy and clap [the class claps one quarter note]. Another is the half note. Everyone clap it with me. Rea-dy and clap." The teacher proceeds with a quick review of dotted half, whole, eighth-note pairs, quarter rest, and the new triplet.

2. "You know all of these, so your job is this: When I say 'go,' you will get in groups of four to five students with whom you can work. Your group will have two minutes to arrange the order of the rhythm cards any way you want. When that is done, you will rehearse clapping the rhythm. After that two minutes, I will give you the next instruction. Quickly and quietly, get ready to form your groups. I will give each group a set of rhythm cards. Go!"

3. The teacher monitors to make sure everyone joins a group and he or she hands out a set of the cards to each group. "Two minutes! [He or she times the students and stops them before they get fidgety and lose focus on the lesson.] Now it's time to rehearse. I will say 'one, two, rea-dy, go,' and you will all perform your pattern together. One, two, rea-dy, go. [The students practice their patterns.] Let's try it once more. One, two, rea-dy, go." They rehearse again.

4. "Now comes the interesting part. Your group will have two minutes to choose *how* you will perform the rhythm. You could use words and perform names of foods or sports, you could use your bodies and perform body percussion, or you could use nonsense words or animal sounds. Whatever you select must be appropriate for our classroom. Two minutes. Rea-dy and go!" The groups make their choices about the performance media and the teacher stops them after two minutes.

5. "The last part of this is that you need to have a leader or conductor for your group. Each group chooses one person to start the group and you'll rehearse your pattern twice. You have one

minute to do this. Go!" The groups proceed and the teacher stops them when he or she hears them finish the second rehearsal.

6. "You've just composed the C section of our piece, so let's have each group perform without stopping in between. I'll begin with Janna's group and point to Mohammad's, Lisa's, and Jim's in that order. Your leader or conductor starts you and you'll perform your rhythm pattern twice. Rea-dy, Janna, and here you go." The teacher cues the other groups to perform in sequence.

7. "That was the C segment. Now we can put our song or A section first, our body patterns or B section next, and our rhythm groups or C section last to create a piece of music that has three different sections. You will need to remember your body pattern from rows 1, 2, or 3. Is everyone ready to do this? Face me and we'll begin with the song." The teacher establishes the starting pitch and lets them sing.

8. "Begin your body movements for B with row 3. Rea-dy and go. [He or she cues row 3, then row 2, and finally row 1 to perform.] We start the C section with the groups, Janna's leading. Rea-dy and go. [The teacher cues each group to begin their performance.] You just did a three-section piece of music, most of which you created or composed. Excellent music making, fourth grade. I'm impressed you could make so many good choices in reading and performing the music and handling yourselves to present your music so well."

Closure and Check of Learning
 "Today we learned a new rhythm."

- Verbalization: Teacher asks a student to tell the class the name of the new rhythm (*triplet*).

- Identification: Teacher asks the class to hold up the number of fingers to show how many sounds are in a triplet.

- Demonstration: Teacher asks the class to perform their body movements to demonstrate triplet rhythms.

- Further application: Teacher asks the students to think about things that appear in threes and that are similar to triplets (to maintain the focus on the concept and expect accountability).

LOTS

Singing the song as a group, moving their bodies, and recognizing differences between steady beat and triplets aurally.

HOTS

Reading, creating, and performing triplets as well as analyzing the listening example to identify the triplets in the context.

The Lesson Model: Grade 4

Concept: *Harmony*, threaded through every segment of this lesson
National Standards:

1. Singing, alone and with others, a varied repertoire of music.

2. Performing on instruments, alone and with others, a varied repertoire of music.

3. Reading and notating music.

4. Listening to, analyzing, and describing music.

5. Evaluating music and music performances.

6. Understanding music in relation to history and culture.

Note: Using baritone ukuleles and/or three-quarter guitars allows both the appropriate size for the children's bodies to accommodate and the interchangeability between instruments since they are pitched alike on the first four strings.

Introduction (Visual and Auditory)
Materials:

- Flashcard with the word *chord* on it

- Piano or other keyboard

- Iconic presentation of a chord with blue, red, and green dashes

- Symbolic presentation of a chord with C, E, and G in blue, red, and green

- The "Row, Row, Row Your Boat" song for the teacher

Procedure:

1. The teacher begins by telling the students what the task is for the day. "Today we are going to stretch your musical brains. To do that we are going to talk about the word *chord*. There are different spellings of the word and different kinds of them such as your vocal *cords* that make sound when you speak or sing; there are extension *cords* that we use to plug into outlets. But the *chord* in music is spelled differently [teacher shows a flashcard with the word on it] and it means two or more sounds that occur at the same time."

2. "We hear chords all the time when instruments are playing together or instruments and singers perform together. For instance, if I play one note on the piano and sing a different note, I've created a chord. This is what a chord looks like." He or she shows another flashcard with an icon of the chord presented as three colored dashes stacked on top of each other; blue is the bottom dash, red the middle, and green the top one.

3. "With the appropriate number of fingers, show me how many *different* sounds will occur in this chord. [The teacher asks the class to predict that three different sounds will occur because there are three dashes of varying colors on the flashcard.] Three is correct. Typically we play three notes together to make a chord."

4. "Listen to three notes played together. [The teacher plays a C and holds it, then adds E, holding it, and finally G, so the class can hear all the sounds enter independently, but resound together.] I am going to sing 'Row, Row, Row Your Boat' [traditional song] and play those three notes so you can hear

my melody with the piano's chord." The teacher sings the melody and plays the C chord throughout the song.

5. "If we use the staff to write our chord, you'll notice that the lowest note sits on its own line. Please blurt the name of that note. . . . Yes, C is correct." The teacher shows another flash-card with middle C notated on the staff in blue, E in red, and G in green to match the iconic version of it.

6. "Let's all sing the C together. [The teacher gives the starting pitch and cues.] One, rea-dy, sing. [The class sings a C until the teacher cues a cut-off.] The middle note of the chord is different. It sits on the bottom line of the staff. Please blurt its name. [The class identifies it as E.] Yes, it's higher than C. Let's sing the E together." The teacher gives the pitch and they sing it.

7. "And the highest note is what? You can blurt again. . . . You are very accurate with G. Sing it with me [he or she gives the pitch and they sing G]. Those three notes form what we call the C chord. It's named for the bottom note. Now we're going to sing the chord together."

Singing (Visual and Auditory)
Materials:

- The "Row, Row, Row Your Boat" song for the teacher

Procedure:

1. The teacher divides the class into three groups, after which he or she sings the tonic and has one group continuously sing the tonic note, taking breaths whenever needed. The third of the chord is sung by group 2, and they sing that note continuously while the fifth is sung by the remaining group. "Please sing your note until you run out of breath, then take a quick breath, and jump right back in until I cue you to stop. This will take a whole minute to do, so be patient. You are singing the C chord while I sing the melody

of 'Row, Row, Row Your Boat' against you. You'll hear my part and your part. Together we will have your chord sung with my melody."

2. Once the class can sing the chord, the teacher sings "Row, Row, Row Your Boat" against the chord to demonstrate melody versus harmony.

Listening (Visual, Auditory, and Kinesthetic)
Materials:

- The "Rocka My Soul" song for the teacher
- Iconic presentation of the C (in blue, red, and green) and G7 chords (in orange, brown, and green)
- Symbolic presentation of the C (in blue, red, and green) and G7 chords (in orange, brown, and green)
- Piano or other keyboard
- Guitar and/or baritone ukulele

Procedure:

1. "Most songs will use more than one chord, so we're going to listen to a song that you already know, 'Rocka My Soul' [spiritual], to determine when the chord changes from C to another one that is called G7. Here is a picture of G7. Notice that it looks different from the C chord." The teacher shows the iconic version of the C chord and that of G7, with the latter having the lowest sound written as a dash in orange, above it the F in brown, and slightly above that the G in green.

2. "With your fingers indicate how many sounds will occur in this chord. Yes, it has three sounds and is called G7. [The students each hold up three fingers.] You are good at predicting the number of sounds! Here is what G7 looks like when it's written on a staff." The teacher shows another flashcard with B [below middle C], F, and G written in orange, brown, and green to correspond with the iconic version.

3. "This is what G7 sounds like [teacher plays B, then F, and finally G, stacking the notes so the class hears each note on its own as it is added to the chord]. You already know how the C chord sounds [the teacher plays it] and now you've been introduced to G7 [teacher plays it]. Listen to it change from C [teacher plays examples] . . . to G7 . . . back to C . . . and then to G7, just like it does in many songs we know."

4. "In a few minutes we are going to play guitars and you'll be learning these two chords. To prepare your ears for this, please practice this with me. I will play these chords and ask you to put a hand on your knee when you hear the first chord, which is C, then put your hand on your head when you hear it change to the other chord, G7. Let's try that." The teacher plays C and reminds them this is the C chord, then changes to G7 and scans the group to make sure they've put their hands on their heads.

5. "You are ready to do this without me. Let's try it. I'll start with C. Show me what you'll do." The teacher plays the C chord and checks for hands on knees, then changes to G7, checking again; he or she moves back and forth between the chords and eventually plays two C chords in a row, then two G7 chords, to test their identification skills.

6. Finally, the teacher switches to the guitar. "Since you are so good at distinguishing between the C and G7 chords on the piano, I'm so curious to see if you can do that when I play them on the guitar [or ukulele]. I'm going to make it trickier, however, because I'm going to sing 'Rocka My Soul' with the two chords."

7. "Show me the C chord with your hands on your knee. It is the first chord. [The teacher plays the chords and sings 'Rocka My Soul' as the students demonstrate their understanding with the hand gestures.] Excellent identification of the chords, fourth grade. I bet that you noticed that my fingers changed when I changed the chords. You are ready for reading the chords on your own."

Moving (Visual, Auditory, and Kinesthetic)
Materials:

- Tape for marking the staff on the floor
- Symbolic presentation of the C chord (in blue, red, and green) and G7 (in orange, brown, and green)
- Recording of "Rocka My Soul"
- Piano or other keyboard

Procedure:

1. There is a floor staff presented with long strips of tape, a staff that has the lines approximately sixteen inches apart so that the students can stand on lines or in spaces. "I will show the C chord flashcard and ask Jerry, Lindsay, and Jeff to make that chord on the staff [the students each assume a position of C, E, or G on the floor staff]. They will stand there for a moment while Alissa, Rique, and Sedra show us the G7 chord on the floor staff [each child takes position for either B, F, or G]. When I hold up the C chord flashcard, the Cs stand up until I change the card; they then squat. When I hold up the G7 card, they stand up, but then squat when it's not their chord's turn."

2. "Everybody will listen to a recording of 'Rocka My Soul' and notice that we switch back and forth between the chords. Please get your listening ears ready." The teacher shows the C flashcard, and plays the recording while changing the cue cards. The students on the floor staff stand during their chord and squat when the other chord is signaled.

3. "I am so impressed that you can listen, change chords, and handle all those sounds at the same time. Let's change people for the chords." The teacher has six other students assume the notes on the staff and then moves to the piano to play the melody and harmony. The class responds.

4. Next, he or she plays the song slightly faster, allowing differ- ent chord changers to respond accordingly and the rest of the class to sing the melody following the teacher's establishment

of the starting pitch. He or she proceeds with this until all the students have had a turn, changing either tempo or dynamics with each turn to maintain their focus. "You have become very adept listeners, for you began to make the switches just before they occurred. You were anticipating the chord changes."

Reading and Writing (Visual)
Materials:

- Slide of the "Rocka My Soul" song

- Projector and screen

- Guitars and/or baritone ukuleles for half the class

- Flashcards of the C and G7 chords

Procedure:

1. The teacher shows the class a poster or slide with the melody and words of "Rocka My Soul" (traditional gospel). He or she asks the class to scan the song and notice the C and G7 chord symbols that sit *above* the staff. "Look at this again and notice the word underneath the staff where the first chord change occurs. Please raise you hand if you can identify that place." The teacher asks a student to physically point to it on the poster or screen.

2. "Yes, the first change occurs on 'rocka,' but where is the next one? Please raise your hand if you know [the teacher has another student point it out]. Yes, it happens again on another 'rocka.' Where is the next one? [A student points to it.] There's a pattern, because it occurs on 'rocka' yet again, but then suddenly switches back on 'soul.'"

3. "We now start the refrain with 'so high, you can't get over it.' When does it change to G7 again? [Another student points to it.] Hmmm. It happens on the 'so low.' Where is the next change? Please blurt the answer. . . . Yes, it's on 'so wide.' The last G7 is tricky. Please blurt the word where we change to G7

for the last time [the class says 'the']. And then we finish on the C chord. You've got it. You've scanned the song to determine the chord changes. You're ready for the guitars and ukuleles."

Performing (Visual, Auditory, and Kinesthetic)
Materials:

- Three-quarter guitars or baritone ukuleles for half the class and the teacher

Procedure:

1. Before the students get instruments, the teacher reviews how to get the instrument and hold it, and then instructs the class to do the following: "Without any sound, you will find a partner with whom you can work. You'll walk to someone, make eye contact with him or her, and that will signify that you're asking him or her to be your partner. That person can either shake his or her head 'yes' or 'no.' If you get a 'no' answer, simply ask someone else. You will get your partners without noise and then sit on the carpet next to him or her by the time I count to five. Five . . . four . . . three . . . two . . . one. Thank you for handling that as I'd asked."

2. "One partner will carefully get a guitar [or baritone ukulele] and rest it on the floor in front of you while the other partner waits for you. [The students get the instruments and return to their spots on the rug.] For today, this half of the class will play the C chord [teacher designates one half] and the other half will play the G7 chord."

3. The teacher shows the tablature for the C chord, demonstrating how to finger it with his or her guitar, and instructs the C group to practice strumming in tempo with him or her. Then the other half is shown the tablature for G7 and the teacher practices with them, strumming together in tempo. The teacher allows this to occur for approximately a minute.

4. "Now switch partners and help your partner find the right chord. Strum with me. Rea-dy and here we go. [The class strums C as

the teacher holds the C cue card and G7 when that card is presented.] Back to the first partner. We're ready for the song. Notice on what chord we start." The teacher slowly establishes the pitch and tempo, singing the song and cueing the chord changes with the cue cards slightly before the change actually occurs so that the students have an instant to "get there" on time.

5. The teacher has the class switch partners and sings it again, moving the tempo only slightly faster to keep them focused and engaged. "You handled the changes quite well and made the song sound as it should. Thank you for watching your fingers carefully."

Improvising, Composing, and Creating (Visual, Auditory, and Kinesthetic)
Materials:

- The "Polly Wolly Doodle" song for the class

- Guitars and ukuleles for half the class and the teacher

Procedure:

1. "Now that you can read and play the C and G7 chords, you get to determine where the chord changes should occur in another song you know, 'Polly Wolly Doodle' [traditional song]. I will hand out the song to partner 1 while partner 2 in each group gets a pencil. Please do that without any noise. Return to your place and be ready to work with your partner."

2. "I see that you're ready. Please listen to the directions. I am going to sing the song and play only the C chord at the very beginning. Your job will be to listen once, then use your own guitar or uke to determine where the chord changes are. You will write a G7 above the staff when it is time to change to that chord and a C when that chord is needed."

3. "Each of you will practice the song twice and then we'll play it together. You have four minutes to do everything." The teacher times the class and brings them to closure when he or she sees that the groups are essentially finished with the task, not allowing any extra "dead" time.

4. "Please rest your instruments and look at me. Partner 2 plays the chords while partner 1 sings. [The teacher gives the starting pitch and sings the tempo cue.] One, rea-dy, sing." After partner 2 has played, the teacher repeats this for partner 1 to do. If there are discrepancies with the chord placements, the teacher will need to sing and demonstrate those places in the song using both chords, allowing the class to decide which is the best fit. "I am impressed that you can hear the chord changes and understand where they belong based on listening to the song. You've just written the chords as a composer does. Nice work, class."

Closure and Check of Learning
"Today we learned two chords."

- Verbalization: Teacher asks a student to tell the class the name of a chord they sang and played today (C or G7).

- Identification: Teacher asks the class to hold up the number of fingers to show how many sounds are typically in a chord (three).

- Demonstration: Teacher asks the class to touch their knees on the C chord and touch their heads on G7 as he or she plays examples on the piano.

- Further application: Teacher asks the students to listen to their favorite music at home and determine when the chords change in that music (to maintain the focus on the concept and expect accountability).

LOTS
Singing the song as a group, singing the chords, and recognizing the number of sounds in the chords based on the iconic presentations.

HOTS
Reading, creating, identifying, and performing the chords.

The Lesson Model: Grade 5

Concept: *Improvisation as related to rhythm*, threaded through every segment of this lesson

National Standards:

1. Singing, alone and with others, a varied repertoire of music.

2. Performing on instruments, alone and with others, a varied repertoire of music.

3. Improvising melodies, variations, and accompaniments.

4. Composing and arranging music within specified guidelines.

5. Reading and notating music.

6. Listening to, analyzing, and describing music.

Introduction (Auditory and Visual)

Materials:

- Flashcard with the word *improvisation* on it

Procedure:

1. "You will enjoy our task today, for you are going to create music and be in charge of that creation. You will probably remember the term that describes making something up on the spot. [The teacher asks for a volunteer to say *improvisation* or introduces the term on a card.] Here is the word. Please say it with me. Im-prov-i-sa-tion."

2. "I could *improvise* the way I walk to the door [the teacher demonstrates an unusual way to walk]. Or Jenna could show you a new way to run to the door [Jenna demonstrates]. That's called improvisation. Class, would you please improvise a new expression on your face and hold it for five seconds? [The teacher monitors the class and times them.] Those were quite different expressions! You are ready to learn more about improvisation, and we will start by reviewing the song we learned last time."

Singing (Auditory and Visual)
    Materials:

- Slide of the "Here We Go, Willowbee" song

- Projector and screen

- Piano or other keyboard

Procedure:

1. "Today we will improvise, but first we need to review a song we learned last week. Please look at the screen and you'll see the song 'Here We Go, Willowbee' [Kenney, 1974b]. I'll give you the starting pitch. Please read it and sing it. [The teacher establishes the starting pitch and cue, playing the song with them on the keyboard.] You read the rhythm and the words accurately."

2. "This time I won't use the keyboard, so make sure your voice is matching the same pitch as everyone else. [Teacher sings the cue on the starting pitch and they sing the song.] Your accuracy was excellent on the pitch matching. Thank you for listening well and matching the pitch."

3. "This is the last time. You'll want to pay close attention to the tricky rhythm on the last part of each verse, for the rhythm changes even though the words remain the same for all three repetitions. [The pitch is established and the class sings again.] Thank you for paying attention to the rhythm. Now that you have good command of the song, you're ready to improvise."

Moving (Visual, Auditory, and Kinesthetic)
    Materials: None

Procedure:

1. "In a moment you will choose a partner and then one partner in each pair will form a line facing the board. The other partner in each pair will be in a line facing the first line, thus there will be two lines facing each other with an aisle in the middle. Nod your head 'yes' if you understand the directions. I'm glad you understand."

2. "Here's how you'll choose a partner. I will pretend I'm asking Andy to be my partner. Without saying a word, I motion back and forth between him and me. He can nod his head 'yes' and we'd be partners or he can shake his head 'no,' in which case I ask another partner. Notice that we do this quickly and begin to form the lines." The teacher pantomimes this and shows where the lines will be.

3. "Class, you have ten seconds to quietly find a partner and get into your lines. It won't matter which line you're in. Rea-dy, and one, two, three. . . . Nice work handling this quickly and quietly. Use your eyes to make sure you're facing your partner."

4. "Here's what we'll do to improvise. Everyone will sing the first verse, 'here we go, Willowbee, Willowbee, Willowbee,' while I go down the aisle. I have to make up or improvise *one* movement that is not walking and not running. Those are boring. We need to be inventive and creative with this. Watch me as I do the moonwalk [or hop from side to side or run backward, etc.] down the aisle. [Teacher demonstrates this.] As I get into my same line at the end of the aisle, everybody performs the refrain by taking a short jump backward and clapping on 'jump back, Susie,' another on 'jump back, Susie,' and another one, and then shimmying forward back to their places on 'all night long.'"

5. "I will go back to the head of the line and do this again. You will sing everything and perform the refrain." Teacher establishes the starting pitch and does the moonwalk [or other preferred movement] down the aisle to the other end of the line while the class sings the first verse and everyone performs the refrain.

6. "Here's the fun part. My partner, Brent, now has to imitate my improvisation, so he'll moonwalk [or other movement] down the aisle during the second verse while we sing 'here comes another one just like the other one' and then he gets at the end of his line while everybody performs the refrain. The next person to lead the improvisation is Lynda and then Jamie will imitate her. Lynda cannot do the moonwalk; we've already used that. She'll need to improvise something else."

7. "You'll need to watch carefully. This is more difficult than it appears." The teacher establishes the starting pitch and cues the class to begin singing while Lynda starts her new improvised move. The teacher continues until everyone in the first line has led the improvisation, telling them that when the class meets again, the other line will lead. "You improvised so well and so quickly, class. Everybody had very inventive moves."

Performing (Auditory, Visual, and Kinesthetic)
Materials:

- Barred instruments with the C pentaton (xylophones, metallophones, and glockenspiels) for half the class

- Appropriate mallets for the instruments

Procedure:

1. The teacher has the barred instruments set up with the C pentaton and mallets available. The instruments are arranged at one end of the room so that the students can walk behind them, sit down, and face the class.

2. "In a moment everyone will be improvising with an instrument. You will all need to stop when I give you the cut-off, so be ready. The second line is going to move behind the barred instruments in a moment and they will use the C pentaton to improvise a *bridge* that we'll insert between the verses of the song. The first line will sit down where you are standing and patiently wait your turn."

3. "Second line, carefully walk around the instruments, behind them, and find a spot to sit so that you are looking directly down at the keys on the instrument. Pick up your mallets when I finish with the directions. Your job is to find a pattern that is eight beats long and one that you can repeat twice. You have one minute to find your pattern and rehearse it two times in a row. First line, you will get unpitched percussion instruments, take them back to your seat, and you'll have forty-five

seconds to improvise your pattern that is eight beats long and is played twice. Handle this without fussing. Please walk."

4. Line 1 gets their unpitched instruments while line 2 is working on the barred instruments. The teacher times them, monitoring to ensure everyone is rehearsing, then presents a large cut-off.

5. "Rest your mallets and instruments. We will need to establish the same tempo. I will count to eight while you *think* your pattern in your head, then we'll play it together. Ready to think. One, two, three . . . eight." Teacher gives cut-off.

6. "Get your mallets and instruments ready. We'll all play our improvisations twice and then stop." Teacher gives starting cue, counting to eight on his or her fingers twice, and then providing a cut-off.

7. "From your places, let's sing 'Willowbee' once, then play the bridge—your pattern twice—then sing the second verse. Your job is to rest your instruments during the singing." Teacher gives starting pitch, cues them, and the class performs. As the first verse is ending, the teacher speaks the starting cue for the instruments as "rea-dy, play."

8. "You handled it expertly, class. I will count to ten while line 1 walks behind the barred instruments and sits down and line 2 walks to the percussion instruments and sits down." The teacher counts while the lines trade places. He or she then repeats the process of improvisation and singing.

9. "Thank you for singing and playing at the appropriate times. Your improvisations worked well with the song and you accurately counted to ensure your playing lasted for sixteen beats. Everyone will put their instruments away and return to your seats without noise. Please do this by the time I count to ten. One, two, three . . . ten."

Listening; Improvising, Composing, and Creating (Auditory and Kinesthetic)
Materials:

- A YouTube video of *4'33"*

- Computer

- A picture of John Cage

- Tape recorder

Procedure:

1. "We are going to prepare to listen to quite an unusual piece of music. This is called *4'33"* and it was written by John Cage, an American composer, in 1952. [The teacher shows a picture of him.] For the entire piece, no instruments are playing and no singers are singing. The music is the natural sound in the room, perhaps someone coughing or a chair squeaking. Please prepare to watch and listen as we see an orchestra with *4'33"* and then we'll create our own piece. You know what to do to listen quietly and without distractions. I'll ask you what you noticed after we finish."

2. The teacher plays the YouTube video (www.youtube.com/watch?v=hUJagb7hL0E), focusing the class on the piece for the first four or five minutes. "So what did you notice in watching and listening to the piece?" The teacher asks three or four students to offer their perceptions.

3. "We are going to create our own piece called *1'30"* and your job will be to make *appropriate* sounds or noises when I cue you do to so and to stop when I move to the next person. You won't have any instruments, so you'll need to be creative with only yourself. We will let everyone in row 3 contribute sounds, then row 2, and finally row 1. We'll record this so that we can listen to it."

4. "Please take twenty seconds to create your *appropriate* sound now and then stop when you see the cut-off. [The teacher monitors the class and times them, giving the cut-off.] Let's rehearse it and record it. Please be ready to start and play when I move next to you and to stop when I move away from you."

5. The teacher begins the recording and cues each student to play for roughly eight beats, cutting off the last sound. "I bet you would like to hear your improvisation. Please prepare to listen

quietly knowing that our next task is to notate the piece on paper. [The teacher plays the recording.] Each of you improvised well and created many different sounds. You watched for cues and gave everyone a chance to contribute. Thank you."

Reading (Visual, Auditory, and Kinesthetic)
Materials:

- Whiteboard, marker, and eraser

- Staff paper and markers for the class

Procedure:

1. "Our next job is to notate the piece that we just improvised so that someone else could perform it. If we take a staff [the teacher has one on the board], we have to find a way to show the length of each sound and the high and low pitches of the sounds. For instance, I might draw a line above the staff to show that Peter whistled a high pitch for five seconds and then let the pitch drop; I draw a squiggly falling line to show the dropped pitch. Alea then growled for eight seconds, so I drew a slightly squiggly line below the staff to show a low pitch."

2. "Please take twenty seconds to play your segment of the piece again and then you'll notate it. I'll give you staff paper and a marker. You'll have one minute to complete the task." The teacher gives a piece of paper with a large staff drawn on it to each student; each paper is numbered to show the sequence of sounds in the piece—that is, that *1* is the first person and *2* is the second person, and so on. The teacher monitors the groups, checks their work, and times them.

3. "Calmly put the caps on your markers, put your markers in the box, and lay your papers on my desk before going to your seats. Juanita, please put the papers in numbered order from one to twenty-five." As the students are cleaning up, Juanita lays the papers on the floor in sequence.

4. "Let's listen to our piece once more and read the notation to see if it is accurate." The teacher starts the recording and then points to the paper as each person's sounds are played.

5. "Tell me if you think our notation was an accurate representation of the sounds. Who would talk about it? Bill, what do you think? [The teacher initiates discussion about this and allows the class to evaluate the accuracy, offering justifications for their comments.] I so appreciate the mature way you handled this today. You were truly thinking about the sounds and describing, creating, and notating the improvisations."

Closure and Check of Learning
"Today we worked with the idea of making up music on the spot."

- Verbalization: Teacher asks a student to share the word that means made-up sounds in music (*improvisation*).

- Identification: Teacher asks the class to look at a song that is written in standard notation and then asks them to identify whether it is composed or improvised (since it has music and lyrics, it is composed).

- Demonstration: Teacher asks the class to recreate their improvised segment of *1'30"*.

- Further application: Teacher asks the students to listen to their favorite music at home and determine if the song is composed or improvised (to maintain the focus on the concept and expect accountability).

LOTS
Singing the song, listening to *4'33"*, and performing the body movements to the refrain of the song.

HOTS
Creating their own improvisations and notating them.

The Lesson Model: Grade 5

Concept: *Lyric composition as related to rhythm*, threaded through every segment of this lesson

National Standards:

1. Singing, alone and with others, a varied repertoire of music.

2. Composing and arranging music within specified guidelines.

3. Reading and notating music.

4. Listening to, analyzing, and describing music.

5. Understanding music in relation to history and culture.

Singing and Listening (Visual and Auditory)
Materials:

- Slide of the "The Battle Hymn of the Republic" song

- Projector and screen

Procedure:

1. The teacher has a slide of "The Battle Hymn of the Republic" prepared and projects it on a screen for the class. "We have a most interesting task to undertake today. You are going to become songwriters, but a special kind of writer in that you're going to write the words or text or lyrics for a song. To musicians, the person who writes the text or lyrics is called a lyricist."

2. "The last time we met you listened to and sang 'The Battle Hymn of the Republic' [music by Steffe and lyrics by Howe]. You recognized that is was a serious song and that its text or lyrics were a bit difficult to understand before we discussed the meaning. Today we are going to create our own lyrics or text and make it far less serious. Let's first take a look at the song and review the original version. Please prepare to listen once more. Your ears are open, mouths and bodies are resting.

Please think the song in your head as you hear it." The teacher plays the recording of the song.

3. "I'll give you the starting pitch and we'll sing this with a slow tempo. [The teacher gives the starting pitch and cue, and plays the keyboard with the class.] You will notice that there are two parts to the song. Use your eyes to identify them. Josh, what is one [verse]? Danika, what is the other [refrain]? Men, please sing the verse and women, the refrain." The teacher gives a starting pitch and cue.

4. "Let's reverse it. Women sing the verse and men the refrain. [The teacher gives the pitch and cue.] You switched parts at precisely the correct places. Since we know the song has a verse and refrain, what is the form of it, Elke? Yes, it is AB. Thank you."

Moving (Visual, Auditory, and Kinesthetic)
Materials:

- The "The Battle Hymn of the Republic" song for the teacher

- Piano or other keyboard

Procedure:

1. "If we begin to analyze this, we find that there are several phrases in the song. In a moment you will be on your feet. When I play a phrase, you will walk in one direction and 'hang in place' on the last word of the phrase; then you will change direction for the *next* phrase, walk it, and 'hang on the last word' by staying in place until the *next* phrase begins, and then change your direction yet again. Your feet will demonstrate the jagged rhythm of the song. The only rules that apply are that your feet must remain on the floor and you cannot touch anybody or anything. If you understand, please nod your head 'yes.' Good. Please stand up without fussing."

2. The teacher plays the song on the keyboard, accentuating the rhythm and lingering on the last note of each phrase in order

to make the point that a phrase has ended and another is beginning. The students walk one direction for each phrase.

3. "Quietly walk back to your chairs in the same manner. I'll play the song once more. [He or she plays it again, but this time it is much softer and the rhythm is less pronounced to allow them to listen more carefully and to calm them.] Thank you for listening carefully and moving to the phrases and the rhythm."

Reading and Writing; Improvising, Composing, and Creating; Performing (Auditory and Visual)
Materials:

- Flashcard with the words *lyrics or text* on it

- Whiteboard, marker, and eraser

Procedure:

1. "Now that we have learned the song and discussed its meaning, we are going to play with it. Our job will be to analyze how the song lyrics were put together in a pattern and then imitate that pattern with another subject for our song. The result will not be a serious song, but rather a humorous one."

2. "Let's look at the number of syllables or word parts for each line of the verse. I'll sing and you count. [The teacher points to the first line of the verse and sings it slowly while the students count.] Rachel, how many syllables are in the first line? Yes, fourteen is correct."

3. "I am going to write the rhythm with long and short dashes so we can see the lengths of the notes for the phrase and then put 'fourteen' in parentheses after the line so that we know how many syllables are needed. Billy, what is the last word of that phrase? You have it. It's *Lord* and I'm going to write it above the last dash so that we see the rhyming pattern in the song."

4. The teacher continues to do this for all phrases of the song, noting that the other lines have fifteen, fifteen, and six syllables in

the verse and eight, eight, and six in the refrain. The rhyme scheme is *Lord*, *stored*, *sword*, and then *on* for the verse and *hallelujah* three times followed by *on* for the refrain.

5. "Let your eyes see the long phrases that end in rhyming words followed by one short phrase that doesn't rhyme in the verse [the teacher does this while pointing to the ends of the phrases as he or she speaks]. And the three short, rhyming phrases of the refrain followed by one that does not rhyme. We need to understand this to make our humorous song."

6. "Today we have to find an appropriate subject for our song and I will propose that we write new lyrics on the topic of school."

7. Note: Be aware of copyright issues for changing lyrics in songs. Whenever not using songs or arrangements that are in the public domain, consult the MENC Copyright Center (www.menc.org/resources/view/copyright-center). Find out how face-to-face teaching activities differ from performing rewritten lyrics for an audience in terms of requiring permission from the copyright holder.

8. "So first we have to generate a list of words that rhyme and could be used, such as *rule*, *cool*, *fuel*, *jewel*, and so on. I will write them as you dictate more. Please give a 'thumbs up' if you have one. [The teacher takes suggestions from the class.] Now we have to return to the syllables and compose lines of text that have the correct number."

9. "I have an example of a similar change to this song that I'll sing for you." He or she demonstrates the song for the class. There are many examples that exist on the Internet.

10. "So the rules are that we (a) maintain the topic of school, (b) compose phrases of the correct number of syllables that end with a rhyming word, (c) and make sure everything we compose is appropriate for school. Let me start the first phrase and end it with a rhyming word from our list." The teacher writes it on the board and sings it for the class—for instance, "My eyes have seen the glory of the opening of school."

11. "Let's clap the rhythm of the second phrase together. Ready, go. [They clap it together.] When you have an idea what should be in that phrase, raise your hand." The teacher takes the dictation from the class, modeling necessary adjustments if needed and having the class sing the song from the beginning as each phrase is added. The teacher will need to draw attention to the differences in phrase length for the refrain and the possible repetition that could occur in three of the phrases.

12. "Now that you've created the entire verse and refrain, let's sing the entire song together. [The teacher establishes the starting pitch and cue.] You utilized the correct number of syllables in each phrase and you adhered to the rhyme scheme. I am very impressed, fifth grade. Good work!"

Closure and Check of Learning

"Today we worked with the idea of composing new lyrics or text."

- Verbalization: Teacher asks a student what is changed to turn a serious song into a humorous one on a different topic (*lyrics*).

- Identification: Teacher asks the class to look at a song such as "America," determine if it is the original or not, and justify the response.

- Demonstration: Teacher asks the class to sing the song they created without his or her help (but he or she establishes the starting pitch and cue).

- Further application: Teacher asks the students to listen to their favorite music at home and determine if the song is the original or not (to maintain the focus on the concept and expect accountability).

LOTS

Singing the song and determining the number of syllables in each phrase.

HOTS

Analyzing the phrases, syllables, and rhyme scheme of the original song and subsequently creating new lyrics or text.

The Lesson Model: Grade 6

Concept: *Ostinato*, threaded through every segment of this lesson
National Standards:

1. Singing, alone and with others, a varied repertoire of music.

2. Performing on instruments, alone and with others, a varied repertoire of music.

3. Improvising melodies, variations, and accompaniments.

4. Composing and arranging music within specified guidelines.

5. Reading and notating music.

6. Listening to, analyzing, and describing music.

7. Understanding music in relation to history and culture.

Introduction
Materials: None

Procedure:

1. "There are elements around us that are repetitive, occurring again and again. We are going to focus on that idea of repetition today, and to begin, let's identify repetition around us."

2. "What comes to mind when you think about something that happens over and over? Raise your hand to name something that repeats." The teacher acknowledges students' responses, such as fences, order of colors in stoplights, ambulance siren's sound pattern, my mother telling me to quit hitting my brother, and so on.

3. "In music that pattern can be extremely important and can exist as many as fifty times in a piece of music. We're going to listen to one of my favorite pieces of music today. It's a song called 'Boomerang' [Covertino, 1986] from the movie *Children of a Lesser God.* Does anyone know what a boomerang is? Yes, it's something that returns to you, so we might suspect that that something is repetitive."

Listening (Auditory, Visual, and Kinesthetic)
Materials:

- Flashcard with the word *ostinato* on it

- Whiteboard, marker, and eraser

- Recording of "Boomerang"

Procedure:

1. "You know what you need to do as we prepare to listen. Please show me you're ready. I will ask you to count the number of times you hear 'boomerang' in the music. Here's a little sample." The teacher plays a few measures to establish the "boomerang, baby" ostinato by the background singers.

2. "That was practice and that you're now ready to identify the number of times it occurs in the song. Please show your good listening manners." The teacher scans the class to ensure they are quiet and focused, then starts the music.

3. "How many times did 'boomerang' occur in the song? Please blurt the answer [thirty-six times]. Who could speak or sing the rhythm of the pattern [*ti ti ta ta ta*]? [Someone volunteers.] Who could go to the board and write the rhythm of the pattern [two eighths and three quarters]? When a repetitive pattern occurs in music, it is called an *ostinato*. [Teacher shows a card with the word on it.] Say it with me. Os-tin-a-to."

4. "Let's clap the ostinato eight times. Read the pattern on the board, please. Rea-dy and go. [He or she cuts them off at the end.] We are going to move to a different ostinato for a challenging game that comes from an old African American street chant. You probably did street chants on the playground when you were younger by speaking something while you clapped and patted a partner's hands. Did you ever do one of those? This one is difficult but I know you will love it."

Moving (Auditory, Visual, and Kinesthetic)
Materials:

- The "My Landlord" song for the teacher

Procedure:

1. "First, let me show you the body percussion ostinato that accompanies this song. The pattern is this: patsch, clap, tap your right hand as if you were touching right hands with a partner, tap left hand as if you were touching left hands with a partner, tap both hands as if you were touching both hands with a partner, cross both hands over your body and touch your own shoulders, and then repeat it."

2. "We're going to try it slowly in the air and get partners later. Let's master this on our own first." The teacher speaks and models the body percussion ostinato as the class is led through it one step at a time.

3. He or she then sings "My Landlord" (Kenney, 1974a) as the class continues to perform the ostinato, allowing the class to hear the song several more times. When the class has command of the ostinato, they are asked to move.

4. "Without making any noise, make eye contact with someone with whom you could be a partner, and with your eyes, ask them. You won't use any words. That person can say 'yes' or 'no' by shaking his or her head. If that person indicates 'no,' you will simply ask another person. Everyone will have a partner and face that person by the time I quietly count to five. Please handle it without any noise [or the teacher must start over and rehearse it with them]. One . . . two . . . three . . . four . . . five."

5. "You should be facing your partner. You will perform the ostinato touching your partner's hands. The trick is that we *stay together* in tempo, so listen and match my speed. Rea-dy and here we go." Once the teacher has established the tempo and class is performing the ostinato, he or she adds the song, repeating it a few times and always maintaining the same tempo.

Singing (Auditory and Kinesthetic)
    Materials:

- The "My Landlord" song for the teacher

Procedure:

1. "Let's add the song to it since you know the ostinato so well. Please face me and keep your good posture for singing." The teacher sings a phrase a cappella and the class echoes. He or she must repair any inaccurate notes, for there are some tricky areas in this song. Once the class has echoed all phrases, he or she sings the entire song for them once more, and they then sing it.

2. When the students have demonstrated command of the song, they face their partners and the teacher begins the counting cue for the body percussion pattern to occur several times before the song is added. The class performs the ostinato and sings, ending with the teacher's cut-off cue. "You did an excellent job of keeping one tempo with the song and working the ostinato pattern with your bodies."

Movement (Auditory, Visual, and Kinesthetic)
    Materials: None

Procedure:

1. The teacher has the class form concentric circles, with one partner in each pair forming an inside circle, shoulder to shoulder, that is facing out. The remaining students face their partners on an outside circle that is facing in.

2. "We are going to pretend that we've just finished singing the song once and performing the ostinato, and at the very end everyone must move to a new partner without losing a beat. The inside circle remains in place while everyone in the outside circle moves one position to their right. The outside circle will do that when I say 'go' and will be in place to start the song with a new partner."

3. "Let's practice. Rea-dy, go! Let's do it again. Rea-dy, go! Now we'll start the ostinato, add the song, and at the very end we'll move to new partners to begin the song again, never stopping in between. Here goes the pattern. One, two, rea-dy, go."

4. A parenthetical remark: I predict, based upon my experience teaching this to my sixth graders in public school and my education and music education majors at the university level, that they will "crash and burn" after the first or second partner switch. My remedy has been that they return to their original partners, I take a slightly slower tempo, and we rehearse it again before returning to the earlier tempo.

5. "We pulled it together after the fourth switch of partners. You remained focused and kept the tempo going. Thank you for your good work."

Improvising, Composing, and Creating (Auditory, Visual, and Kinesthetic)
Materials:

- Barred instruments (three xylophones) and temple blocks
- Appropriate mallets

Procedure:

1. "Since you are very familiar with an ostinato, you are going to work in groups to create an ostinato to further accompany 'My Landlord.' One group will create an ostinato for the baritone xylophone, one for the alto xylophone, one for the soprano xylophone, and one for unpitched percussion on the temple blocks."

2. "We will need to determine how many beats the body percussion ostinato is and match your ostinati to that. While I perform it, please count how many beats it is." The teacher demonstrates it and the class determines it is eight beats in length. He or she assigns groups to create their eight-beat ostinato with their instruments, expecting that everyone in the group will contribute and handle it without any issues, and gives them two minutes to

complete the task. He or she monitors the groups and watches the clock, stopping as they finish.

3. "It's time to share your ostinato patterns. Each group will perform its ostinato with one person as the designated instrument performer and the others performing through clapping or patsching. It will be crucial for everyone to remain at the tempo of the song. Group 1, rea-dy and here you go. [The teacher physically cues each group to begin and cut off.] Excellent performance, class. You maintained the tempo and didn't miss a beat."

Reading and Writing (Auditory, Visual, and Kinesthetic)
Materials:

- Large staff paper and markers

- Whiteboard, marker, and eraser

- Barred instruments and temple blocks

- Appropriate mallets

Procedure:

1. "In each group there will be a scribe who will notate the ostinato on large staff paper. While the scribe works, the responsibility of the rest of the group is to assist him or her and check the accuracy. Try clapping the ostinato by reading the pattern on the paper. Your groups have two minutes to accomplish this."

2. The teacher hands out the paper and utensils, then times the class to complete the task. He or she cuts them off just as they are appearing to finish.

3. "In your groups, determine another partner who can be the conductor, a person who can start and stop the rehearsal of the pattern. Find that person by the time I count to ten. One, two . . . ten. [The groups make their own decisions.] The conductor will put his or her group's notation on the board and will then lead all of us in performing it. You will need to count it

and cut us off. Please take one minute to rehearse your own group's ostinato twice." The teacher monitors the class and cuts them off as they finish.

4. "Tina, please put your ostinato on the board and have everyone start with you to play it. You will count and cue them to enter." The teacher has the conductor from each group lead the rehearsal of each pattern, one at a time.

5. "Another person in your group must perform the pattern four times so that we can layer the ostinato patterns on top of each other. Jonah's group begins, then Harry's, third is Sheena's, and fourth is Toby's. Once you enter, play your pattern until I give everyone a cut-off. That could be many times of repetition, so be prepared. Get prepared. Rea-dy and here we go." The teacher layers the patterns on top of each other, allowing the last group to play a minimum of four times, then cuts them off.

6. "You are ready to do this with the song. The fourth person in each group will play the ostinato, beginning with Cho's group, and will continue as long as it takes to sing the song. I will then cue you to stop playing one group at a time until only Rita's group is left to play the ostinato four times. Rea-dy and here we go."

7. The teacher layers in the ostinati, allowing each group to play the pattern four times before the next is added. He or she cues the class to sing, then cuts off the ostinati one pattern at a time, the last group having played four times before stopping. "You did a fabulous job of watching my cues. Everyone performed together and we made wonderful music!"

Performing (Auditory, Visual, and Kinesthetic)
Materials:

- Barred instruments and temple blocks

- Appropriate mallets

Procedure:

1. The teacher divides the class into the following: One person from each group is on an instrument, and the remainder are in their concentric circles, ready for performance. He or she cues the body percussion ostinato to begin, then adds the instruments in one at a time.

2. The class performs the song, moving to a new partner at the end, but this time the teacher stops after the move has occurred and reassigns the instrument players to shift one instrument to their right. The remaining person moves back into the outer circle at a designated place and a new person moves from the outer circle to the baritone xylophone (tape on the floor indicates the "new" instrument member's trail to the instrument and another line of tape for the "returning" instrument player to leave the instrument and move back into the circle).

3. There are designated places where the move occurs so that the students are not confused. The teacher restarts the performance and stops them after the circles have changed partners. He or she repeats the process, shifting everyone to another instrument and tells them that the next move means everyone shifts without stopping the song. The song is repeated several times, allowing the outer circle to have played instruments and performed in the circle.

Closure and Check of Learning
"Today we learned about a repetitive pattern in music."

- Identification: Teacher asks the class to listen to around thirty seconds of "Boomerang" and one student will speak or sing the ostinato from the song.

- Verbalization: Teacher asks one student to define *ostinato* and another to give an example of a repeating pattern that occurs somewhere outside of music class.

- Demonstration: Teacher asks the class to clap the ostinato he or she played on the instruments.

- Further application: Teacher asks two students to bring a recording of a song that demonstrates ostinato to the next music class and to be prepared to teach what it is, where it occurs, what instruments or voices are responsible for the ostinato, and how many times it occurs in the song. This is a form of assessment that can be recorded by the teacher, but he or she will need to continue similar assignments across many classes to accommodate everyone.

LOTS

Recognizing and counting the ostinato pattern in "Boomerang"; singing and performing the body percussion ostinato with "My Landlord."

HOTS

Creating and performing the new ostinati on the instruments to fit with the song.

The Lesson Model: Grade 6

Concept: *The twelve-bar blues form, using chord roots*, threaded through every segment of this lesson

National Standards:

1. Singing, alone and with others, a varied repertoire of music.

2. Performing on instruments, alone and with others, a varied repertoire of music.

3. Improvising melodies, variations, and accompaniments.

4. Composing and arranging music within specified guidelines.

5. Reading and notating music.

6. Listening to, analyzing, and describing music.

7. Understanding music in relation to history and culture.

Note: Before this lesson, the students should have ample exposure to and experience with singing chord roots. This can be accomplished by singing a song that does not change chords. The song is then accompanied by singing the tonic (*do*) by the teacher and eventually the students. After proficiency has been achieved, the third and fifth of the chord may be added at the teacher's discretion. This process is then extended to songs with a clear dominant chord change.

The teacher can sing or play an instrument without changing chords, and he or she will lead the students to realize that another note is needed (*so*). As before, the third and fifth can be added after the students are comfortable. This process is extended to songs with clear dominant and subdominant chord changes, and the teacher would lead the students to use the notes *do, fa*, and *so* appropriately as accompaniment. Throughout this process, the students would visually, auditorily, and kinesthetically practice chord roots and chords using various melodic instruments such as voices, pitched percussion, or recorders.

Additional note: For the purposes of this lesson, the twelve-bar blues form will be used for learning. Typically, the twelve-bar blues form is as follows (four beats or one measure per chord):

I   I   I I
IV   IV I I
V(7) IV I I

Introduction (Visual, Auditory, and Kinesthetic)
    Materials:

- Recording of the "Every Day I Have the Blues" song

Procedure:

1. "As you find your seats, listen for any repeated phrases in this song. [The teacher plays a recording of 'Every Day I Have the Blues' (King, 1994).] If you can identify a repeated phrase, raise your hand." The students answer that the first line is repeated in every verse.

2. "Let's do our physical warm-up according to the form of the text. Using As and Bs, who can tell us the form of each verse?" A student answers, "AAB." The teacher plays the recording and gives several examples of varying body stretches that fit the form, such as stretch up, stretch up, stretch down.

3. As time allows, the students may suggest various movements that match the form. This process may be extended to vocal warm-ups or breath exercises as well. "You handled the AAB form of the stretches perfectly. Let's explore more about this form."

Singing (Auditory, Visual, and Kinesthetic)
Materials:

• Recording of the "Good Morning Blues" song

Procedure:

1. "Let's see if the form of the text of this song is the same or different." The teacher plays a recording of or performs "Good Morning Blues" [Ledbetter, 1996]. The students answer, "It's the same, AAB."

2. "Musicians call this type of music the blues. Many blues songs' texts fit the AAB form. Let's see how well the tonic note fits as an accompaniment for the first verse. Give me a 'thumbs up' when it sounds acceptable to you, and give me a 'thumbs down' when it doesn't sound correct. Please sing *do* throughout and indicate if this fits the tonic with your thumbs." The teacher establishes the pitch and cues the class to sing as he or she plays and sings the song again. The students identify the chord changes aurally and signal with their thumbs.

3. "Let's check our work with the other verses. [The teacher plays and sings additional verses until the students are accurately matching their hand movements to the AAB form.] Based on the songs with *do* as tonic, what note do you think we should use for the first change?" The students answer either "*fa*" or "*so*."

4. "Let's see which one sounds best." The teacher proceeds by playing and singing the song with both notes for the first change. The teacher leads the students to hearing that *fa* sounds better for the first change, the IV chord.

5. "What root will we go to after *fa*?" The students listen and answer "*do*." The process is repeated with aurally identifying the V7 chord root, *so*.

6. "I'll play and sing the song again, and you sing the roots from my hand signs. [The teacher establishes the pitch and cue, then the students sing the roots.] Thank you for accurately singing what the hand signs indicated. This is a very typical form of the blues."

Reading and Writing (Visual and Kinesthetic)
Materials:

- A twelve-bar progression lead sheet

- Paper and pencils

- Recording of the "Good Morning Blues" song

Procedure:

1. The teacher prepares his or her example of a twelve-bar progression lead sheet, guiding the students to simulate this. "Jazz and blues musicians sometimes don't read music like we've read music this year. They use a kind of shorthand version called lead sheets."

2. The teacher shows an example of a guitar, piano, or bass lead sheet, with the slashes representing beats with chord changes over the measures. "This makes it easier to sight-read a new song at a practice or even a gig. A gig is a musical event such as playing for a concert or for listening in a restaurant during a meal or making music on the street."

3. "Let's make our own lead sheets for the blues form we've been discussing. Quickly and quietly get your writing materials and return to your seats. You have until the count of ten, then freeze where you are. One, two . . . ten." The students collect their paper and pencils, then return to their seats.

4. "Unfreeze and let's sing one verse of 'Good Morning Blues' and conduct to figure out the time signature." The teacher sings and play the song while the students conduct and identify that it is in 4/4 time.

5. "Raise your hand if you know how many beats should be in each measure. Daniella, what is the number? Yes, four is precise. How about the kind of note that gets one beat? Robert, what note is that? Yes, it is a quarter note. Class, please blurt the time signature that should go at the very beginning of our blues lead sheet. [The students answer that the time signature is 4/4.] Add a 4/4 time signature to begin our first line." The students place a 4/4 in the top left portion of their papers.

6. "Let's listen to one verse and find out how many measures there are. Please count the measures by one–two–three–four, two–two–three–four, and so on as we've practiced before." The teacher plays and sings the song, and the students identify that there are twelve measures in the first verse.

7. "Musicians call this form the twelve-bar blues because it has twelve measures or bars. They just repeat this pattern over and over for the whole song. What note from our hand signs should we put for the beginning [*do*, or tonic]? Gabrielle, what is the first note? Exactly! *Do* is the first note."

8. "Let's see how long we stay on the tonic. Count the measures and raise your hand when it changes. [The students listen again and raise their hands in the fifth measure.] Since we're in 4/4 time, how many slashes should we put in each measure? Please blurt the answer. Yes, there are four. On your paper put four measures of four beats, using slashes and bar lines, to form the first line." The students add slashes to represent beats and add bar lines to create the first line of the form.

9. "Now let's do the second line. Who remembers what note we move to following *do*? Helena, what is the new note? Correct. It is *fa*. Let's see how long we stay on *fa*." The teacher plays and sings the verse, and the students identify that there are two measures of *fa* and then a change.

10. "Listen again and determine what note change occurs after *fa* and how long we stay on the changed note. [The teacher plays and sings the verse again.] What note did we change

to after *fa*, Jon? You correctly identified *do*. How long do we now stay on *do*, Miguel? Yes, for two measures."

11. The teacher continues this process for the final line with *so*, *fa*, and *do* so that the students have three lines of four measures each. "Let's sing from our notation. [The students sing the twelve-bar blues pattern using hand signs.] I'm impressed at how well you sang the correct pitches and matched the hand signs."

Performing (Visual, Auditory, and Kinesthetic)
Materials:

- Barred instruments

- Appropriate mallets

Procedure:

1. "Now let's play the twelve-bar blues on the classroom instruments. Taking your lead sheet, quickly and quietly move to the barred instruments and get your mallets ready for playing." The students move to instruments and prepare to play as they have been previously taught. The pitched percussion instruments should be set up for a C pentachord (*do–re–mi–fa–so*).

2. Depending on students' previous experience, the teacher can either transfer the root progression to absolute note names— that is, the musical alphabet—or continue to refer to the notes in solfège.

3. "Let's play and sing our twelve-bar blues progression using the barred instruments. On the instruments, which note is *do*, Gretchen? Yes, it's C. Class, if *do* is C, play the note one time that is *fa*. Rea-dy and go. [The students play F.] F is correct. If *fa* is F, play *so* just once. Rea-dy and play. [The students play G.] Thank you. You now have the pattern of *do*, *fa*, and *so*."

4. "Let's play the roots using our lead sheet for the form. For now, let's just play one note per beat. Let me sing the pattern of the first line to demonstrate. [The teacher sings *do* four

times.] Your turn to play the lead sheet. Rea-dy and here we go." The students sing and play the twelve-bar pattern while the teacher conducts in 4/4 with pronounced downbeats.

5. "Now let's put some 'bluesiness' in the pattern. Play this uneven rhythm. It's very uneven. [The teacher demonstrates a swing rhythm of dotted eighths and sixteenths on each beat.] Class, join me on C. Rea-dy and here we go." The students join in after a few measures to continue with the form. The class practices several times with only the twelve-bar pattern.

6. "Now let's sing 'Good Morning Blues' while we accompany ourselves. [The teacher establishes the starting pitch and cue.] You were able to keep the beat, rehearse the rhythm, play the correct roots, and sing all at once. Excellent music making, class."

Improvising, Composing, and Creating (Visual, Auditory, and Kinesthetic)
Materials:

- Barred instruments

- Appropriate mallets

Procedure:

1. "In a moment we'll add another element to your lead sheets. You're going to take your paper and pencils with you. I'll give you seven seconds to find a group of four with whom you can work well. Be on time. One, two . . . seven, and sit down. Everyone, focus your attention on the directions."

2. "You can use one person's paper to do this, so let the others rest for a while. You will compose *text* for a blues song that fits our twelve-bar blues form and the AAB form of the text. Compose a chorus that will repeat, and then two or three verses that go along with it."

3. "You can use the melody from 'Good Morning Blues' or you can come up with your own. You only have eight minutes. Remember that all text must be school-appropriate." The teacher

monitors the class and observes when they seem to finish, redirecting them immediately.

4. "Now choose some percussion instruments and barred instruments to accompany your group. Decide how many will play, but know that everyone has to help sing. Please get the instruments now." The students get instruments and decide who will play them.

5. "I'll give you two minutes to practice your composition with your group, then you'll perform for the class. Make sure someone in your group gives a starting cue." The students practice their compositions several times.

6. "Let's perform by group. Bill's group, please get ready to perform. Everyone else needs to focus attention on his group and be a respectful audience. [Each group performs and the teacher comments specifically about each.] Thank you for creating such interesting pieces. You made excellent decisions in writing text and adding accompaniment today."

Listening (Visual, Auditory, and Kinesthetic)
Materials:

- Recording of the "Walk On" song

Procedure:

1. "Carefully return your instruments where they are stored and go back to your seats. You've got seven seconds. One, two . . . seven." The students return their instruments while the teacher counts to seven.

2. "We're going to listen to another twelve-bar blues song that fits our form. It is called 'Walk On' [Watson and Holt, 2002]. I will ask you to listen to see which instrument or instruments were playing alone and see if the voices use the same form as the instruments. Silently show your hand signs while you listen. Let's see if you can do the form by memory."

3. The teacher cues them in tempo and the students follow the twelve-bar pattern using hand signs while they listen. "Adrianne, did you hear any instruments playing alone? [She says, 'Yes, the guitars.'] Raj, what pattern do you think the other musicians used to accompany the solo? [He says, 'Twelve-bar blues.'] Was it the same for the voices, Heidi? [She says, 'Yes.'] Musicians can sing, play solos, or even play in groups as long as they know that they're playing the twelve-bar blues."

Moving (Auditory, Visual, and Kinesthetic)
Materials:

- Recording of the "Hound Dog" song

- A picture of Elvis Presley

Procedure:

1. "You're going to show me that you've got the twelve-bar blues pattern memorized by moving to it. In the 1950s, some musicians used the blues as a foundation for a new kind of music, rock and roll. One very famous early rock-and-roll musician was Elvis Presley [teacher shows a picture of Presley], and he had a lot of popular songs then."

2. "Please stand up in your place. Let's listen to one and use our hand signs to check and see if it's twelve-bar blues." The teacher plays "Hound Dog" (Presley, 2002) and the students use hand signs as before to check the pattern.

3. "Please stand in your places. Without touching anyone else, step the beat of the song in one direction at the beginning. When the root changes, you have to change directions to match the twelve-bar blues pattern. The rules for this are that you cannot touch anybody or anything and your feet must remain on the floor, but you can step in any direction you like to demonstrate the root changes. Let's try it."

4. The teacher plays the recording and the students experiment with changing directions as the progression occurs. "You iden-

tified the beat very quickly. Thank you for following directions and changing your directions to match the form."

Closure and Check of Learning (Visual, Auditory, and Kinesthetic)
"Today we learned about a pattern used in blues music."

- Identification: The teacher asks the class to name the pattern that was studied today (*twelve-bar blues*).

- Verbalization: The teacher asks students to mention the number of root notes in the twelve-bar blues (three roots), and to name the other style of music that was based on the blues (*rock and roll*).

- Demonstration: The teacher asks a student to lead the class in singing the roots of the twelve-bar blues using the hand signs; he or she then asks another student to sing the group's repeated section of their composition.

- Further application: Teacher asks students to bring a recording of a song that demonstrates the twelve-bar blues pattern to the next music class and to be prepared to identify what instruments or voices are used for the pattern and how many times the pattern repeats. This is a form of assessment that can be recorded by the teacher, but he or she will need to continue similar assignments across many classes to accommodate everyone.

LOTS

Identifying chord roots and solfège; performing solfège using instruments and voice.

HOTS

Analyzing the music to determine chord root changes and the form, determining the pitch levels of the roots, and creating the twelve-bar blues composition using voice and instruments.

REFERENCES

Abeles, H. F., Hoffer, C. F., and Klotman, R. H. (1994). *Foundations of music education* (second ed.). New York: Schirmer Books.

Barbe, W. B., and Milone, M. N. (1980). Modality. *Instructor, 89*(6), 44–47.

Barbe, W. B., and Milone, M. N. (1981). What we know about modality strengths. *Educational Leadership, 38*(5), 378–380.

Barbe, W. B., Swassing, R. H., and Milone, M. N. (1979). *Teaching through modality strengths: Concepts and practices.* Columbus, OH: Zaner-Bloser, Inc.

Bargar, J. R., Bargar, R. R., and Cano, J. M. (1994). *Discovering learning preferences and learning differences in the classroom.* Columbus, OH: Ohio Agricultural Curriculum Materials Service (ERIC Document Reproduction Service No. ED401311).

Bergethon, B., Boardman, E., and Montgomery, J. (1997). *Musical growth in the elementary school* (sixth ed.). Fort Worth, TX: Harcourt Brace College Publishers.

Bizet, G. (n.d.). *Classical series—program notes: L'arlésienne excerpts.* Retrieved May 5, 2010, from www.daytonphilharmonic.com/content.jsp?articleId=845.

Bloom, B., Englehart, M., Furst, E., Hill, W., and Krathwohl, D. (1956). *Taxonomy of educational objectives: The classification of educational goals. Handbook I: Cognitive domain.* New York: Longmans, Green & Co.

Boardman, E. (2001). Generating a theory of music instruction. *Music Educators Journal, 88*(2), 45–53.

Bruner, J. (1966). *Toward a theory of instruction.* Cambridge, MA: Harvard University Press.

Carder, P. (Ed.). (1990). *The eclectic curriculum in American music education: Contributions of Dalcroze, Kodály, and Orff.* Reston, VA: MENC.

Carlsen, J. C. (1973). Concept learning: It starts with a concept of music. *Music Educators Journal, 60*(3), 34–37, 99–102.

REFERENCES

Choksy, L. (1981). *The Kodály context: Creating an environment of musical learning.* Englewood Cliffs, NJ: Prentice-Hall.

Choksy, L. (1988). *The Kodály method.* Englewood Cliffs, NJ: Prentice-Hall.

Choksy, L., and Hein, M. A. (1978). *The singing book: Beginning level.* San Francisco: Renna/White.

Collett, M. J. (1991). Read between the lines: Music as a basis for learning. *Music Educators Journal, 78*(3), 42–45.

Consortium of National Arts Education Associations. (1994). *National standards for arts education: What every young American should know and be able to do in the arts.* Reston, VA: MENC.

Covertino, M. (1986). Boomerang. On *Children of a lesser god* [CD]. Los Angeles: Crescendo Records, Inc.

Dunn, R. (1993). Learning styles of the multiculturally diverse. *Emergency Librarian, 20*(4), 25–32.

Eisner, E. (2000). Benjamin Bloom, 1913–99 [Electronic version]. *Prospects: The Quarterly Review of Comparative Education, 30*(3). Retrieved September 3, 2008, from www.springer.com/education/journal/11125. In V. Ordonez (Ed.), *Open File: Education in Asia* (pp. 387–395). Brussels, Belgium: UNESCO Subscription Service.

Elliott, D. J. (1995). *Music matters: A new philosophy of music education.* New York: Oxford University Press.

Hodges, D. A. (2000a). Implications of music and brain research. *Music Educators Journal, 87*(2), 17–22.

Hodges, D. A. (2000b). Music and brain research: Sweeter music all the time. *Education Digest, 66*(3), 39–54.

James, W. B., and Galbraith, M. W. (1985). Perceptual learning styles: Implications and techniques for the practitioner. *Lifelong Learning, 8*(1), 20–23.

Kassner, K. (2009). Reflections on career development and eclecticism in music education. *Music Educators Journal, 96*(1), 62–66.

Kenney, M. (Ed.). (1974a). My landlord. In *Circle round the zero.* St. Louis: Magnamusic-Baton, Inc.

Kenney, M. (Ed.). (1974b). Willowbee. In *Circle round the zero.* St. Louis: Magnamusic-Baton, Inc.

King, B. B. (1994). *Blues on top of blues.* London: EMI.

Krathwohl, D. R., Bloom, B. S., and Masia, B. B. (1964). *Taxonomy of educational objectives: Handbook II: Affective domain.* New York: David McKay Co.

Labuta, J. A., and Smith, D. A. (1997). *Music education: Historical contexts and perspectives.* Upper Saddle River, NJ: Prentice Hall.

Ledbetter, H. (1996). *Where did you sleep last night: Lead Belly legacy, Vol. 1.* Washington, DC: Smithsonian Folkways.

Marks, J. (n.d.). *Rudolph, the red-nosed reindeer.* Retrieved May 5, 2010, from www.snopes.com/holidays/christmas/rudolph.asp.

Merriam-Webster. (2010). Thread. *Merriam-Webster's Online Dictionary.* Retrieved September 2, 2009, from www.merriam-webster.com/dictionary/thread.

Miller, B. A. (2002, Winter). Touch the music! Learning modalities in elementary music class. *General Music Today, 15*(2), 4–13.

Mosolov, A. (1926–1927). *About the piece: The iron foundry.* Program notes by Laurel E. Fay (April 2007). Retrieved May 5, 2010, from www.laphil.com/philpedia/piece-detail.cfm?id=1607.

No Author. (2005). I have a car. In *Share the Music, Grade 3.* New York: McGraw Hill.

Paxcia-Bibbins, N. (1998, Spring). Listening with a whole mind: Holistic learning in the music classroom. *General Music Today, 11*(3), 11–13.

Persellin, D. C. (1992). Responses to rhythm patterns when presented to children through auditory, visual, and kinesthetic modalities. *Journal of Research in Music Education, 40*(4), 306–15.

Pierpont, J. L. (1967). *Jingle bells.* Chicago: Rubank, Inc.

Presley, E. (2002). *Elvis: 30 #1 hits.* New York: BMG.

Regelski, T. A. (1983). Action learning versus the pied piper approach. *Music Educators Journal, 69*(8), 55–57, 64.

Regelski, T. A. (2004). *Teaching general music in grades 4–8: A musicianship approach.* New York: Oxford University Press.

Reimer, B. (2003). *A philosophy of music education: Advancing the vision* (third ed.). Upper Saddle River, NJ: Prentice Hall.

Restak, R. (1979). *The brain: The last frontier.* New York: Doubleday.

Rubin, R. (1988). Have you seen my honey bears? In *Holt Music, Book 1* (E. B. Meske, M. P. Pautz, B. Andress, and F. Willman, Eds.). New York: Holt, Rinehart and Winston.

Sanders, P. D. (1996). Perceptual modality and musical aptitude among kindergarten students. *Contributions to Music Education 23,* 89–101.

Simpson, E. J. (1966). *The classification of educational objectives, psychomotor domain* (Report No BR-5-0090). Washington, DC: U. S. Department of Health, Education, and Welfare (ERIC Document Reproduction Service No. ED010368).

Steffe, W., and Howe, J. W. (2005). Battle hymn of the republic. In *Making music, grade 5.* Glenview, IL: Pearson Education, Inc.

Tchaikovsky, P. I. (2005). Trepak. In *Making music, grade 3.* Glenview, IL: Pearson Education, Inc.

Trinka, J. (1989a). *John, the Rabbit.* Eagan, MN: Folk Music Works.

Trinka, J. (1989b). Lady, Lady. In *John, the Rabbit.* Eagan, MN: Folk Music Works.

REFERENCES

Trinka, J. (1996). *The Little Black Bull, Volume 4.* Eagan, MN: Folk Music Works.

Watson, D., and Holt, D. (2002). *Legacy.* Fairview, NC: High Windy Records.

Willis, M., and Hodson, V. K. (1999). *Discover your child's learning style.* New York: Three Rivers Press.

Wilson, V. (1996, November). *Scholars, active learners, and social butterflies: Preferred learning styles of high school biology I students.* Paper presented at the Annual Meeting of the Mid-South Educational Research Association, Tuscaloosa, AL.

Wong, H. K., and Wong, R. T. (2005). *The first days of school.* Mountain View, CA: Harry K. Wong Publications, Inc.

Wood, A. (1992). *Quick as a cricket.* Singapore: Child's Play International.

ABOUT THE AUTHOR

Debra Gordon Hedden is an associate professor of music education at the University of Kansas in Lawrence. She earned a bachelor's degree in music from the University of Iowa, a master's in music education from the University of Northern Iowa, and a doctorate in curriculum and instruction with an emphasis in music education from the University of Northern Iowa. She has been recognized as an outstanding teacher in Iowa by MENC and the Iowa MEA; has been noted as an accomplished teacher in MENC's *Teaching Music*, October 2000; and has received various teaching awards at the University of Northern Iowa. She teaches graduate and undergraduate courses in music education and founded the University of Kansas Youth Chorus (KUYC), in which both undergraduates and graduates work with her in conducting weekly choral rehearsals. Hedden has served as past chair of MENC's Society for General Music, as a member of the Ad Hoc Committee on Undergraduate Curriculum Reform for the Orff-Schulwerk Association, and as a member of the editorial boards for the *Bulletin of the Council for Research in Music Education* and the *Journal of Music Teacher Education*. In addition to writing MENC's General Music Curriculum Framework Document and publishing articles in numerous music education publications, Hedden has presented at conferences in the United States and around the world and has conducted numerous choral festivals in Kansas, New York, Wisconsin, and Iowa.

Breinigsville, PA USA
11 November 2010
249141BV00002B/1/P

9 781607 094418